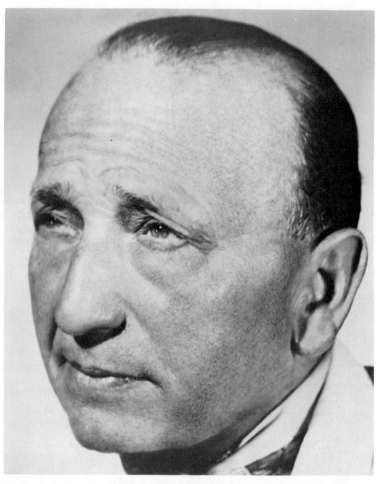

A portrait of Michael Curtiz taken during production of THE PROUD REBEL in 1958.

The American Films of
MICHAEL CURTIZ

By Roy Kinnard
and R.J. Vitone

The Scarecrow Press, Inc.

Metuchen, N.J., and London

1986

Library of Congress Cataloging-in-Publication Data

Kinnard, Roy, 1952-
    The American films of Michael Curtiz.

    Filmography: p.
    Includes index.
    1. Curtiz, Michael, 1888-1962--Criticism and
interpretation. I. Vitone, R.J. II. Title.
PN1998.A3C895 1986   791.43'0233'0924   86-969
ISBN 0-8108-1883-3

Manufactured in the United States of America

ACKNOWLEDGMENTS

I wish to thank the following individuals who, giving generously of their time, advice, and loan of materials, contributed
to this book: Al Bielski, Danny Burk, Ted Okuda, Joseph
Savage, Maurice Terenzio and Ed Watz.

TABLE OF CONTENTS

<u>A note to the reader</u>:

In the text, the numbers in parentheses (after film titles)
refer to cast and credit entries in the filmography.

A Biographical Introduction

In recent years, the old Hollywood studio system, which breathed its last in the late 1950s, has fallen into disrepute. Most of today's films, we are told, are much better and offer, during production, far more creative freedom than the movie factories of the past ever did.

There is some truth to these assertions. Studios had very definite limitations. Film-makers of days past were tied to their respective studios by long-term contracts. Their visions were compromised by censorship, their concepts restricted by budgetary limitations and tight shooting schedules, their scripts and actors chosen in advance for them by insensitive producers more interested in fast profits than in artistic quality. At times, censorship approached idiocy in its restrictions. A cookie-cutter, assembly-line mentality frequently resulted in films that were little more than puerile tripe, and financial corner-cutting on "B" pictures often all but destroyed whatever possibilities a script offered.

But in earlier films, there was also a strong continuity of product, a sense of history, a high level of technical expertise. Most of all (and in the last analysis, probably most important), there existed a simple, honest desire to <u>entertain</u> the public.

These qualities aren't found very often in movies anymore--a fact borne out by the large numbers of people staying away from theatres. And there are fewer movies being made now. Those that do appear cost their backers increased individual expenditure and risk. The producers of these films increasingly "play it safe" in their choice of subject and style, aware that the odds against any particular movie becoming a success--either creatively or financially--grow higher and higher.

Ask people what their favorite movies are; the age of

each person asked doesn't matter. Chances are good that
some of the titles mentioned will be of films from the studio
era of the '30s and '40s--titles like The Adventures of Robin
Hood, Angels with Dirty Faces, The Sea Hawk, Yankee Doodle
Dandy and Casablanca. Besides being classics, these films
have one more thing in common--they were all directed by the
same man, Michael Curtiz.

Curtiz, who directed under contract to Warner Bros.
for nearly three decades after a successful early career in
European silents, was the ultimate company man. He was the
studio system, and, during his remarkable half-century career
in film, he was largely responsible for the successful construction of some of the greatest movies ever made. Associating
with many of the most talented performers and technicians the
industry had to offer, Curtiz worked in every film genre.
Nearly everyone, at one time or another, has been entertained
by a Michael Curtiz film.

Because he was so tangled in the studio system, and
because he directed so many films, the prolific Curtiz is often
labeled a "hack" by those who denigrate mere "entertainment."
To be sure, not all of his movies are great (nor, on the other
hand, could they be, considering the speed and economy employed in their production), but the number of good--and even
superlative--films that Curtiz directed is staggering--78 (known)
European silents and 100 American features from 1926 to 1961!
Certainly a man who entertained so many so well deserves, if
not total respect, then at the very least an appreciative nod.

●   ●   ●

"I put all the art into my pictures I think the audience can
stand."

--Michael Curtiz

●   ●   ●

Curtiz was born Mihaly Kertesz in Budapest, Hungary,
on December 24, 1892. His family was poor. His father was
a carpenter. In addition to Mihaly, there were four daughters and three other sons. Curtiz first entered show business
at the age of 14 when his family moved to Vienna; there he
became a theatrical extra, acting in mob scenes of plays.

Obviously infatuated with performing, Curtiz joined a traveling circus two years later, and, as a trampoline artist, he
spent the next three years touring Europe. The 19-year-old
Curtiz then invested his accumulated savings in studies at
the Austro-Hungarian Royal Academy of Theatre and Art,
where he eventually found employment as an actor in both
classical and contemporary dramas produced in Budapest and
in other major European cities.

Around this time, Curtiz made his first contact with the
film industry, which paid him less than fifty dollars a week
to be an actor. Like many theatrical actors, however, Curtiz
found emoting for the camera to be less than satisfying, and
soon he turned to directing.

Stimulated by his new profession, he traveled to Sweden,
where he applied for a position at Swenska Biograph Studios.
There the prestigious director Joseph Sistrom hired Curtiz as
an assistant, and, by the middle of 1914, Curtiz was a full-
fledged director. This period marked the beginning of movies
as a major form of entertainment, both in Europe, and in
America where D.W. Griffith had already made The Birth of
a Nation. The creative and financial potential of film was obvious, at least to those already at work in the new industry.

But as soon as Curtiz began to advance in Swedish
films, World War I exploded in Europe, and the young director immediately enlisted in the Austro-Hungarian artillery.
Toughened by his lean early years, he was athletic and a
good horseman.

For three years, until serious battle wounds relieved
him from combat, Curtiz served on the Russian front. His
professional film experience was then put to good use when
he was assigned to a division that became one of the first
military units to make wartime propaganda films. The com-
munist revolution that followed ended his military service.
Returning to the commercial film industry, Curtiz worked for
two years at UFA studios in Berlin, where his fellow directors
were the likes of Fritz Lang and Ernst Lubitsch.

Shortly before this move, Curtiz had married Lucy Do-
raine, a 17-year old aspiring actress who began appearing in
his films (they were later divorced in 1923). He continued
to grow in expertise and stature at studios throughout Europe

(Sascha Films, in Budapest; Cinema Eclair, in Paris; and
Torino, in Italy), returning to UFA for a brief time. He
also worked at Gaumont-British in London, where he became
particularly skilled directing huge crowds during action
pictures and Biblical epics.

In 1926, while on a business trip in Europe, Jack
Warner's brother Harry saw Curtiz' film Die Slavenkonigan
(later released in America as Moon of Israel). The film,
which was based on H. Rider Haggard's novel and influenced
to no small extent by DeMille's The Ten Commandments
(1923), deals with the story of Moses and depicts the part-
ing of the Red Sea. Deeply impressed with Curtiz' directorial prowess, Harry advised Jack to screen a print. After
seeing the film, Jack Warner signed Curtiz to direct for
Warner Bros. at a starting salary of $180 per week; this
was more money than Curtiz had been earning, at the time,
in Europe.

In his autobiography, My First Hundred Years in
Hollywood (Random House, 1964), Jack Warner recalled
Curtiz' arrival in America:

> Harry promised Curtiz press conferences and a
> gala reception in New York, and instructed him to
> memorize a short speech in English. As the steamer
> slid up the Hudson River to the dock there were
> fireboats hurling spears of water high above the
> ship, there was a band playing martial music on
> shore, and the sky was on fire with Roman candles
> and bursting rockets. Mike was so overcome that
> he wept. "Ah, thees America!" he cried. "Vot a
> vunderful velcome for the great Michael Curtiz. Und
> these Varner Brothers! I love all five at vunce!"

According to Warner, brother Harry then corrected
Curtiz on the proper number of Warner brothers (four), but
didn't have the heart to tell the new arrival that the "welcome" had, in reality, been a Fourth of July celebration.

Arriving at Warner Bros. in Hollywood, Curtiz quickly
established himself as a studio workhorse. He became a
quick, reliable, no-nonsense director, who often went to
great lengths to insure authenticity in his films. On one
early gangster picture Curtiz, reportedly, spent a good deal

of time in courtrooms and in the offices of the Los Angeles
District Attorney, where he studied the criminal milieu. He
even got permission to pose as a felon and serve a weekend
in jail. To prepare for a western set in Texas, Curtiz read
every book he could find on that state's history.

A stickler for detail as well as for visual innovation,
the hardworking director was frustrated, during his early
years at Warners, by the often immobile camera. In an effort to obtain more fluid and effective shots, he experimented
a great deal. While shooting The Gamblers in 1929, Curtiz
positioned his camera and operator on a treadmill in order to
achieve a traveling zoom effect. When Jack Warner saw this
scene in progress during shooting, he didn't understand
what Curtiz was trying to achieve and ordered him to stop.
In the screening room, however, Warner was pleased with
the results and ordered the studio's other directors to study
Curtiz' techniques.

Working long hours on the set--often refusing to eat
lunch--Curtiz expected the same kind of dedication from his
cast and crew. A tyrant to his co-workers, he often, in
his zeal to obtain good results, was shamefully neglectful of
safety precautions. (The reports of injuries suffered by actors and animals on the sets of Noah's Ark and The Charge
of the Light Brigade scandalized the industry.) Many performers and technicians disliked Curtiz intensely. Frequently, he was embarrassed when his fractured English and
misuse of the language was quoted (usually with glee) by
the press. ("What are they trying to make from me, a
jingle bells?" he once asked a writer.) Many of the infamous
malaprops attributed to Samuel Goldwyn actually originated
with Curtiz.

Long-married to his second wife, writer Bess Meredyth,
Curtiz maintained a low social profile; he had only a few
friends in the business. One of them, producer Hal Wallis,
once described how Curtiz, who was hosting a dinner party
at the Curtiz ranch, began rearranging guests and food at
the table. Appearing always to be visualizing, even when
he was not at the studio, Curtiz was working out a dinner
party scene he was to shoot the next day.

As a result of directing major stars like James Cagney,
Bette Davis, and Edward G. Robinson, as well as from dis-

covering new ones like Errol Flynn, Curtiz' reputation grew. His prestige increased throughout the '30s and early '40s, hitting its peak recognition in 1942 when he directed Casablanca (for which--after several previous nominations-- he was finally awarded an Oscar for Best Director).

After the mid-'40s, Curtiz entered a long period of gradual decline; his films, though still displaying workman- ship, became less impressive. He was working with major stars, his importance to Warner Bros. had not decreased, but the quality of the scripts he directed (seemingly with less and less interest) had diminished.

In the late '40s, Curtiz formed his own production unit within Warner Bros. The agreement allotted him direct financial interest in his films. But, in 1953, rather than accept a pay cut required by a studio economy move, Curtiz left Warner Bros. after making more than 80 features, dur- ing more than a quarter of a century in their employ.

In his last years, Curtiz directed more than a dozen films for other studios. Some of them are surprisingly im- posing works, considering that they were made by a man in the twilight years of his career. The Comancheros, a well- done and enjoyable western, starring John Wayne, was Curtiz' last film. Curtiz died of cancer on April 11, 1962.

Apparently somewhat a ladies' man despite his long second marriage, Curtiz had divorced his wife Bess Meredyth a year before his death, and he was, according to Jack Warner, "...the only director in history who, after his death ... was adjudged the father of an illegitimate child." Whatever controversies or scandals surrounded Curtiz, though, the fact remains that he entertained millions with his skill and craftsmanship.

His films, at their very best, exhibit a flair and un- pretentious artistry rare in movies (or any art form for that matter). Vivid atmosphere, well-modulated performances, and striking visual compositions are the considerable rewards available to anyone who watches one of Michael Curtiz' better films of the '30s and '40s. He was, indeed, as actor Paul Henreid (Casablanca) once said, "Among the top seven, or so, directors of all time." Author John Baxter said in his book Hollywood in the Thirties (A. S. Barnes & Co., 1968):

"Inescapably one of the best directors ever to emerge in the cinema, Michael Curtiz lays a substantial claim to being one of the greatest directors of the thirties."

But perhaps Curtiz himself provided his own best epitaph when once he pontificated on his goals as a director: "To make the best pictures I can that will give audiences their money's worth; to please myself as much as I can without forgetting that the pleasure of my audiences comes first. Thus only do I think I can make any substantial contribution to the art of motion pictures."

The Early American Features

The silent film era was drawing to a close in 1926, the year
Curtiz was directing his first picture for Warner Bros. The
plot of this first film, The Third Degree (79), was a trite
one, set against a circus backdrop. It involved a mother
eloping with a man who is eventually paid to disrupt her own
daughter's marriage, years afterward.

Mordaunt Hall, the film critic for The New York Times,
didn't think much of the script, but in his review of
February 15, he did have slight praise for Curtiz' direction.
Commented Hall: "The narrative is not so well finished as
it might be and the direction and cinematic effects have evi-
dently been inspired by E. A. Dupont's masterpiece
Variety, but even an imitation of Variety is apt to be infi-
nitely more entertaining than drivel in its original form."
The star of The Third Degree was Dolores Costello, who was
married to John Barrymore (under limited contract to Warners
at the time); she was to appear in several more of Curtiz'
early films for the studio. Apparently Curtiz' mettle was
being put to the test by the Warners brass as he put Miss
Costello through her paces before the cameras.

Curtiz' second film (also starring Dolores Costello)
was A Million Bid (80). The picture was a variation of the
tried and true "Enoch Arden" theme, which concerns a
woman who marries a surgeon after her first husband is
apparently killed in a storm, only to find after her second
marriage that her first husband is still alive. The critics
were even less kind to this film than they had been to The
Third Degree. Said Mordaunt Hall in his New York Times
review of May 31:

> Michael Curtiz, a Viennese director who drew atten-
> tion to himself by his orgy of pictorial dissolves in

his film version of The Third Degree, once more
amuses himself by photographic stunts in his new
film A Million Bid. While some of Mr. Curtiz' ideas
are interesting they do not fit into this current of-
fering as well as they did in the cinematic version
of Charles Klein's play. There are parts of this
subject that are virtually lifeless and other sections
that are quite bright.

Next, in 1927, came The Desired Woman (81), starring
Irene Rich as an officer's attractive wife living in the midst
of love-starved soldiers at a desert fortress in the Sahara;
the title tells the rest of the story.

Again, Mordaunt Hall of The New York Times had
mixed feelings about a Curtiz picture. In his review of
August 30, he said:

> This ditty of the desert, in which romance has not
> been omitted, is concerned with a British company
> of soldiers, and Michael Curtiz, the director, does
> put into his production some authentic atmosphere
> in the way of correct uniforms and the British
> salute. He is not to be congratulated, however, in
> having a wide-eyed officer staring through a window
> at the Captain's bride or on other incidents that
> take place.

Good Time Charley (82) was Curtiz' next project. It
is the drama of a song and dance man, starring future
"Charlie Chan" Warner Oland. Again the reviews were less
than enthusiastic. Mordaunt Hall said in his New York
Times critique of November 21:

> While Michael Curtiz, an expert in odd camera angles
> and compelling dissolves, has introduced some inter-
> esting photographic ideas in his latest production
> Good Time Charley, the story of this film teems with
> cheap sentiment and extravagant comedy. The inci-
> dents are handled in an extremely haphazard fashion,
> so that, under the circumstances, almost anything
> might happen. There is a fund of material in this
> subject, but little of it is effective. It is like using
> a bludgeon to bring tears and explosives to create
> laughter.

Noah's Ark: George O'Brien and Dolores Costello.

In 1927, The Jazz Singer, starring Al Jolson, revo-
lutionized the film industry with the advent of sound.
Studios scrambled aboard the talkie bandwagon, and many
silent movies already in production were hurriedly revamped
to include sound sequences. Curtiz' Tenderloin (83), released March of 1928, was one such hybrid effort. A drama
about a thug who is rehabilitated by a nightclub dancer

(Dolores Costello), the picture again failed to please Mordaunt
Hall. He reported in his March 15 review that "...the spec-
tators were moved to loud mirth during the spoken episodes
of this lurid film."

Up to this point, pictures assigned to Curtiz had been
relatively insignificant in subject matter. Production trap-
pings were routine, although the direction, at least, had often been singled out as a point of interest.

Curtiz' next project, released in March of 1929, was
anything but insignificant and routine, and the magnitude of
the production demonstrated the growing confidence that
Warners had in Curtiz' abilities. Darryl Zanuck, who would
go on to helm Twentieth Century-Fox in the mid-'30s, had
joined Warners in 1928, vowing to produce "the greatest picture ever made."

The result of that statement, one year later, was
Noah's Ark (84)--a part-talkie. Like nearly every other
Biblical film produced at that time, Noah's Ark was heavily
influenced by D. W. Griffith's Intolerance and DeMille's The
Ten Commandments in that it contained a modern sequence
used as a parallel counterpoint to the Biblical segment. The
stars (Dolores Costello and George O'Brien) and many of the
key featured actors played dual roles, theoretically making
the "moral" that much more acceptable to a wide audience.
The modern story, taking place in World War I and high-
lighted by an impressively staged train wreck, was of less
interest than the Biblical segment dealing with Noah and the
great flood, for which Curtiz supplied dazzling visuals involving huge masses of extras and immense sets. During
the flood sequence, a huge tank, containing more than half
a million gallons of water, was constructed with access spill-
ways leading to the tops of a Babylonian temple set. After
the contents of the tank were released into the set, extras
and stuntmen thrashed about for the 15 cameras recording
the scene. Due to the lack of adequate safety precautions,
many injuries resulted, including one (unconfirmed) death.

Cameraman Hal Mohr had objected to this dangerous
scene while he and Curtiz were blocking it out before
shooting. But Mohr's objections were ignored. Curtiz,
speaking of the stuntmen and extras who would be involved,

Noah's Ark: Dolores Costello (center) plays a dual role in
the modern World War I sequence.

reportedly had answered flippantly: "They're just going to
have to take their chances."

        A rightfully outraged Hal Mohr walked off the produc-
tion in disgust before the scene was shot, and the photography was completed by Barney McGill.

        Despite Curtiz' impressive direction and huge budget
allotment, Noah's Ark was a failure with the public and with
the critics, especially.   Alvah Johnson of The New Yorker
called it "an idiotic super-spectacle with parallel Old Testa-
ment and Jazz Age sequences--Moses against Scott Fitzgerald
... widely conceded to be the worst picture ever made."
The critic for The New York Post opined: "A solid bore,
with a very second-rate war story in which everything from
The Big Parade to date has been shabbily copied."   And
Mordaunt Hall of The New York Times said that the picture

"frequently borders on the ridiculous ... after sitting through this cumbersome production, one feels that it is a great test of patience." If anyone connected with Noah's Ark was affected professionally by its failure, it wasn't Curtiz; he continued with his regular directorial assignments. Noah's Ark, minus the sound sequences--and with a newly dubbed music and sound effects track added--was reissued in 1957.

The Glad Rag Doll (85), a rich boy-show girl romance, was followed by Madonna of Avenue A (86), a murder story set in a night club; The Gamblers (87) is an unusual drama dealing with the stock market; Hearts in Exile (88) is a Siberian love story, which was filmed with two alternate endings; Bright Lights (89) is a tale of smugglers; and, River's End (90) deals with a criminal who impersonates a Mountie out to capture him.

In 1930, Curtiz helmed what was to become his most commercially successful (if not exactly his most directorially impressive) picture to date. Incorporating Technicolor sequences for some of the musical numbers, Mammy (91), re-leased in April and starring Al Jolson, was well received by critics and the public. This was Jolson's fourth feature. The actor's popularity would soon peak and begin to wane, but this eventual slackening would be less Jolson's fault than the studio's.

After Jolson's tremendous success in The Jazz Singer, Warners seemed to believe that all the public wanted was to see him in the same, tired, "mother love" type of plot. Mammy is no exception, despite its backstage murder mystery angle.

Jolson's acting was trying at times (his "drunk" scene in Mammy, excruciating), but his singing was so dynamic that the screen could barely contain him.

Curtiz managed to establish a detailed show-business atmosphere as we watch Jolson's traveling minstrel act move from town to town. But in other scenes, strangely listless and paralyzed nondirection allows the picture to lapse into tedium. Possibly, the egocentric Jolson clashed with the equally abrasive Curtiz, who simply threw in the directorial towel. Nevertheless, the popular and critical success of

A Soldier's Plaything: Harry Langdon (center).

Mammy enhanced Curtiz' reputation. The film was followed
by Under a Texas Moon (92), a western romance involving
the adventures of two Mexicans in the title state. The
movie was filmed in Technicolor. It featured Frank Fay,
Raquel Torres, and Myrna Loy (four years away from starring in The Thin Man) in a supporting role.

    Curtiz' A Soldier's Plaything (93), an amusing pro-
grammer with some admirably directed sequences, is primarily
noteworthy as silent screen comedian Harry Langdon's first
sound feature. Langdon, a major attraction in full-length
films like The Strong Man (1926) and Long Pants (1927),
both directed by Frank Capra, gradually lost popularity as
he veered away from his audience and directed himself in a
trio of self-indulgent, mordant comedies. By 1929, he was
appearing in a series of genuinely poor "comeback" two-
reelers for Hal Roach. Due to the introduction of sound
film and the talkie-hungry public's clamor for anything
audible, these movies, surprisingly, bolstered his career.

Though he had signed a long-term contract, Langdon, in April of 1930, requested to be released by Roach in order to take advantage of a Darryl Zanuck offer to co-star in a Warner Bros. feature, tentatively entitled Easy Go. Ben Lyon received top billing. He was a polished--if nondescript-- leading man, who between various assignments was still being called for retakes on Howard Hughes' Hell's Angels. Lotti Loder, Noah Beery, and Jean Hersholt rounded out an interesting cast for what was intended to be Warner's answer to the popular Victor McLaglen-Edmund Lowe wartime come- dies being made at Fox. Production began under Curtiz's direction in May of 1930.

The film opens at Coney Island in 1917 as war is de- clared on Germany. Otto (Harry Langdon), an American of German descent, immediately enlists in the allied cause. His streetwise pal Georgie (Ben Lyon) thinks Otto is crazy to volunteer, yet he finds himself following suit in order to es- cape from a gangleader's bodyguards, believing he has actually killed the thug in a brawl. After a melodramatic beginning played in a fairly straightforward manner by both leads, the film becomes an episodic series of comedy turns dominated (to good effect) by Langdon.

Curtiz apparently had the foresight to make sure that Harry Langdon's dialogues were integrated with visual humor. The problem with Langdon's first sound shorts was grounded in the lack of sympathy inherent in Harry's role as "little boy lost." Langdon was a visual comic. His sight-gag range virtually began and ended with his face, so his continuous and irrelevant chatter, during those earlier films, dispelled the intimacy he had established with moviegoers. In A Sol- dier's Plaything, the dialogue is pointed; it is also utilized prudently whenever Langdon indulges in a pantomimic routine.

Langdon's funniest sequence involves a variation on the "awkward squad"; Langdon never speaks a word and carries the scene entirely with gestures. Executing a smart "About face!," he finds himself staring nose to nose at a soldier. Ordered to "Present arms!," Harry offers the other soldier a handshake. Instructed that the troops will "swim through muck and mire" if necessary, Harry gyrates like a fish, all the while remaining poker-faced.

An episode with Lyon and Langdon gallivanting in a
horse costume and upsetting traffic borders on the sur-
realistic. In contrast, Harry's encounter with a deaf French
girl is rather poignant (until Harry divulges his yearnings
by showing the lass a French postcard!). In the film,
Langdon also plays the piano and sings a hilarious novelty
song, "If You Will Oui-Oui Me, I'll Oui-Oui You." During
this performance, he climbs atop the piano and acts sultry
à la Dietrich.

Particularly in the early episodes celebrating America's
entry into the war, A Soldier's Plaything reveals painstaking
technical care. As Lyon loses himself in a crowd of army
volunteers, the orchestration of mounting patriotism is
handled with greater finesse here than during parallel sequences in Warner's The Public Enemy, made the following
year.

Although A Soldier's Plaything was completed and
ready for release in the fall of 1930, it did not receive general distribution until April of 1931. By that time Harry
Langdon's second sound feature, the disastrous Universal
production, See America Thirst (1930), had already been released and was sounding the death knell to Langdon's short-
lived comeback. In Thirst, Langdon resorted to his
"babbling idiot" persona of the Roach two-reelers, system-
atically undoing any possible good achieved in his first sound
feature.

Before its release, A Soldier's Plaything was scaled
down to program feature length (a mere 57 minutes), leaving
many scenes dangling in midair; in fact, one subplot involving Jean Hersholt was removed entirely. Hersholt appears
in one shot only, where he has a single line of dialogue.
Potential comedy routines (Langdon's encounter with a stage
dummy) are not long enough and have little opportunity to
develop. The arbitrary cutting disrupts the flow of the
film, transforming a believably motivated beginning into slap-
stick comedy. Critics who bothered to review A Soldier's
Plaything dismissed it as slapdash. But the care lavished
on sets and crowd scenes suggests that the film is really a
fascinating curio. This being the case, Curtiz may have
created a major early '30s comedy-drama, only to have it
truncated and effectively scuttled by big-studio policies.

Curtiz' next group of films included The Matrimonial Bed (94), a marital comedy-drama starring Lilyan Tashman; Daemon des Meeres (95), the foreign-language version of Lloyd Bacon's Moby Dick, and completely refilmed by Curtiz with a German-speaking cast (shooting separate foreign versions of movies, rather than simply dubbing, was a common studio practice at the time); a Joan Blondell drama titled God's Gift to Women (96); The Mad Genius (97) with John Barrymore, a disappointing takeoff on Barrymore's Svengali, which had been directed by Archie Mayo the same year; The Woman from Monte Carlo (98), a story about a naval wife (Lil Dagover) who is cheating on her officer husband; Alias the Doctor (99), which stars Richard Barthelmess as a physician accused of malpractice (this picture was co-directed by Lloyd Bacon); and, The Strange Love of Molly Louvain (100), which concerns a girl (Ann Dvorak) who is courted by three men.

With these films, Curtiz was just beginning to hit his stride. At age 40, after having directed 100 features in Europe and America, Curtiz would have his best films still before him; the first of three horror films was one of them.

Doctor X (101)

In 1931, the movies <u>Dracula</u> and <u>Frankenstein</u>, both from
Universal, had been huge popular and critical successes, and
these pictures had promptly set a precedent for horror films.
Every major Hollywood studio jumped on the bandwagon;
Paramount with <u>Dr. Jekyll and Mr. Hyde</u>, MGM with <u>The Mask
of Fu Manchu</u>, and so on. Many of these films, with their
imaginative lighting, visual composition, and set design influenced by flamboyant subject matter, have since become
classics.

At Warners, <u>Svengali</u> followed quickly in the wake of
<u>Dracula</u> and <u>Frankenstein</u>. John Barrymore starred in the
title role. Archie Mayo directed the film, which benefited
greatly from the Barrymore style and the striking expressionistic sets of designer Anton Grot.

Expressionism, stemming from the German silents of
the 1920s, was a natural ingredient of the horror film.
During the sound era, it was brought to America (although
in a gentler and more palatable manner) by technicians and
artists who were mostly European immigrants; many of them
had originated the style in Europe. (Karl Freund, for in-
stance, photographed such German silents as <u>Metropolis</u>, and
later piloted the cameras for <u>Dracula</u> in America.)

Expressionistic horror was accepted easily at Universal,
where many of the employees were German and the tastes of
management leaned towards Gothic subjects. At Warners, too,
though perhaps to a lesser extent, expressionistic horror
found a home. This was not surprising, considering that
Curtiz and Anton Grot were under contract there. Curtiz
explained his approach to directing horror films in an inter-

view published in the exhibitor's pressbook for <u>Mystery in
the Wax Museum</u>. That film was released six months after
<u>Doctor X</u>, but, because the two films are similar in style,
content, and plot structure, Curtiz' remarks are applicable
to both pictures:

> Odd, unusual camera angles should never be used
> for their own sake although the temptation to do so
> is often great, especially to the man who has an
> aptitude for thinking in them. The only reason for
> using an angle, in presenting a scene that would not
> seem the usual one to the onlooker, is to obtain a
> definite effect upon the spectator, which can be
> gained in no other way. You wish to arouse at that
> point a feeling of surprise, of terror, of repulsion,
> of admiration--and to emphasize it, the person or
> thing you are photographing must be presented from
> a special angle. Otherwise the natural, straight-
> forward method of recording a scene in pictures is
> the one that holds the spectator's interest, keeps the
> story moving and preserves the flow and tempo of
> the action. It is very easy, in a story like <u>Mystery
> of the Wax Museum</u>, for instance, to overdo the use
> of bizarre, startling angles. That is why I used
> them throughout the picture sparingly, and always
> with a definite purpose in mind. Unless one is
> chary of the employment of them, their effect is very
> quickly blunted, and thereafter they become a
> nuisance instead of a help. Much more effective is
> the specialized type of lighting we used to establish
> and build up a mood that we wished to communicate
> with the spectator. This was particularly true of
> the sequences laid in the two wax works--the London
> one and the New York museum. In each, without
> being too obvious in our lighting, we tried to arouse
> in the spectators' minds a vague, intangible feeling
> of uneasiness, mystery, a sinister something lurking
> in the shadows, never shown but only suggested.
> The use of color is an asset in creating such moods
> in a story of this type. To be sure, stories of the
> fantastic, the horrible, the bizarre have been told
> with fullest success in black and white photography.
> But it has always been a question in my mind whether
> those very stories would not have been more gripping,
> more realistic, if they had been photographed in

color such as we have employed with such unusual
success in Mystery of the Wax Museum and Doctor X.

One must take the (often fabricated) material contained
in studio pressbooks with a grain of salt, to say the least.
And, assuming this was an oral interview, it is difficult to
imagine Curtiz, who was infamous for his broken English,
presenting his theories with such eloquence. However, there
is enough solid reasoning in this dissertation to indicate
that at least the gist of the interview represents a faithful
statement of the director's creative technique. If Curtiz
had made Doctor X at Universal, his directorial methods
would have been put to the acid test since a good portion
of that studio's output consisted of horror films. At
Warners, though, the usual picture during this period was
deeply rooted in the contemporary urban scene, the fast-
talking Cagney gangsters and social commentary seemingly
torn from big-city newspaper headlines. On the rare oc-
casions when Warners attempted a horror film, the studio
usually ran into trouble--the demands of style clashing with
the harsh reality of company policy. Warner Bros. Svengali,
and the film's lesser spin-off The Mad Genius (also with
Barrymore, and directed by Curtiz) had been typical
"period pieces"--despite the occasional intrusion of a modern
auto. They avoided any lengthy contact with modern reality,
the stylized sets and photography leaving no doubt as to the
mythic and romantic intent of the films.

Difficulties arose, though, when the studio adapted
Doctor X from a mystery play by Howard W. Comstock and
Allen C. Miller. The story's main character is a wisecracking
newspaper reporter who is investigating a series of murders
committed during the full moon--the trail eventually leading
to a group of suspects at a medical research institute. The
urban character of the reporter and the unavoidably modern
setting presented serious problems in sustaining the atmosphere so necessary to the success of horror stories. To
bail themselves out of their creative dilemma, the scriptwriters
followed the only viable way open to them and stuck their
tongues firmly in their cheeks.

Doctor X opens with hotshot reporter Lee Taylor (Lee
Tracy) on the fog-enshrouded trail of the mysterious "moon
murderer." To date, the assassin has claimed several victims, and, if true to his established modus operandi, is due
to claim another one soon.

Doctor X: Fay Wray (left) lies unconscious in the hooded
monster's arms as Lee Tracy (right) attempts to save her.

Unknowingly, as he stakes out the city morgue hoping
for a break in the story, Taylor himself is menaced by the
hooded killer, but he escapes unharmed and then sees promi-
nent physician, Doctor Xavier (Lionel Atwill), arrive at the
morgue with several policemen. Deciding to investigate,
Taylor hides in the morgue, covering himself with a sheet
and posing as a corpse. Thus concealed, he is all ears as
Xavier examines the remains of the moon murderer's previous
victim and deduces that the wounds on the body are in all
probability the work of a professional surgeon. The police
immediately suspect one of Xavier's medical associates at his
research institute.

Taylor decides to investigate Xavier. He goes to
Xavier's isolated research facility, and is caught by Xavier's
daughter Joan (Fay Wray) when he tries to break in; an icy
relationship develops between them. The police, convinced
that Xavier knows more about the killings than he is telling,

are also at the institute. Several of Xavier's medical col-
leagues are established as likely suspects, and Xavier,
wishing to avoid any unfavorable publicity, vows to unmask
the killer himself if the police will only give him enough
time.

In a bizarre attempt to reveal the murderer, Xavier
employs a creative tactic. He restages one of the killer's
most vicious crimes as the suspects watch, each man connected to a machine that measures his pulse rate. Supposedly, the reenactment of the murder will excite the guilty
party, and his accelerated heartbeat will serve as his "con-
fession." As the charade proceeds, with Joan playing the
victim strapped helplessly to a bed, the real killer enters--
not the servant who was supposed to have played the role
in Xavier's reenactment. The hideously deformed maniac
threatens the terrified and helpless Joan and reveals himself
to be Wells (Preston Foster), who has not previously been
suspected because he is an amputee, missing one hand.
Wells reveals that he has discovered the secret of "synthetic
flesh." Using this substance, he is able to disguise his
face by completely altering his features and replacing his
missing hand with a living, fully operational appendage. As
Wells continues to strangle Joan, Taylor appears from a
hiding place nearby and attacks the monster. A fierce
battle ensues in the corridors of the mansion, and Taylor
gains the upper hand. He sets the monster ablaze with a
tossed kerosene lamp, and the fiend stumbles through a
window, falling to his death on the cliffs below.

While Curtiz brought to Doctor X the atmosphere that
the film needed, the scriptwriters imbued the film with a
flaky sense of humor that, incredibly, works to the picture's
distinct advantage. If viewers expect from Doctor X a
"serious" horror film along the lines of Frankenstein, certainly they are disappointed. It is only when the movie's
serio-comic approach is anticipated that it becomes a very
entertaining film indeed.

Certainly, intentional humor has been attempted in
horror films many times since Doctor X. But these attempts
are seen mostly in the form of heavy-handed "camp," which,
by trying to make alleged "sophistication" accessible to a
mass audience, flattens out into a "style" that is really no

style at all. In contrast, Doctor X plays like a nutty, very
unpretentious, and very likeable comic book.

      Doctor X marked the horror film debut of Fay Wray,
who would, of course, star in King Kong the following year.
A former Paramount contract player, Miss Wray had been assigned mostly ingenue roles by that studio, despite the fact
that she had been very effective in The Wedding March,
directed by Erich von Stroheim. When the ingenue type
passed out of style in the early '30s, Fay Wray, along with
Mary Brian, was released from the Paramount roster. In
Doctor X (perhaps at Curtiz' direction), she began to project a more alluring image, and the change was noted by
reviewers as an improvement. Fay Wray is very appealing
in Doctor X, as she would be in her other horror films.
So strong, in fact, is her appeal in horror films, she is
remembered primarily for her work in that genre, even
though she appeared in only a half-dozen pictures of that
type during her long film career.

      Today, although original 35 mm Technicolor prints do
exist, Doctor X is, unfortunately, available for television
and non-theatrical showings only in black-and-white. The
film does not depend on the use of color as frequently or
as effectively as Curtiz' similar Mystery of the Wax Museum
(q.v.), but some scenes are obviously much more dynamic
in that medium. The Return of Doctor X, a 1939 "B" effort
directed by Vincent Sherman and featuring Humphrey Bogart
as a vampire(!), bears no connection to Doctor X, even
though the title deceitfully implies a sequel.

•   •   •

Doctor X was followed by Cabin in the Cotton (102), with
Bette Davis and Richard Barthelmess. This drama about
Southern sharecroppers finds the Barthelmess character
nearly led to ruin by plantation vixen Davis (Davis to
Barthelmess: "Ah'd love to kiss ya, but Ah jes' washed
mah hair") and remains engaging even today. 20,000 years
in Sing-Sing (103), a hard-bitten prison drama that teamed
Spencer Tracy and Bette Davis for the first and only time,
is an impressive effort. Utilizing an almost semi-documentary
style this picture criticizes the nation's penal system. In
the process it allows Tracy (excellent as the main convict)
to demonstrate that James Cagney wasn't the only actor

capable of handling this type of role. Portions of the film's
narrative falter under clumsy writing--particularly in the
second half--but even after decades of prison movies, 20,000
Years in Sing-Sing has lost none of its punch.

Mystery of the Wax Museum (104)

Curtiz' Doctor X, released in August of 1932, was a considerable success riding, as it did, the crest of the horror movie
wave. But by the beginning of 1933 the horror craze was
beginning to wane. There had been a glut of such films.
As good as most of them had been (and are, many having
attained classic status), audiences were tiring of them, and
the critics, seemingly out of spite, were being less than
kind in their appraisals. A considerable market, however,
still existed for such pictures, and Warners assigned Curtiz
the task of directing a follow-up to Doctor X. What he produced, released in February of 1933, was Mystery of the
Wax Museum (known simply as Wax Museum while in production).

Obviously aware that the market for horror movies
had contracted somewhat, the studio apparently was trying
to insure success by reassembling as many members of the
well-remembered Doctor X production team as possible.
Lionel Atwill and Fay Wray were reteamed; Thomas Jackson
even was brought back for a brief role.

The two films are very similar in plot and treatment.
Both have a newspaper angle, with the Lee Tracy reporter-
hero of Doctor X given a distaff slant for Mystery in the
person of Glenda Farrell.

Lionel Atwill plays, with eye-gleaming relish, sculptor
Ivan Igor, a man horribly burned and crippled when his
wax museum in London is destroyed by arson (so that Atwill's
sponsor can collect on the insurance). Twelve years later,
Atwill has set up shop again in New York. His assistants
sculpt his exhibits for him because his charred hands are
useless.

In the meantime, spunky news-hound Glenda Farrell
is investigating a series of incidents involving missing per-
sons, stolen bodies from the morgue, and a horribly deformed

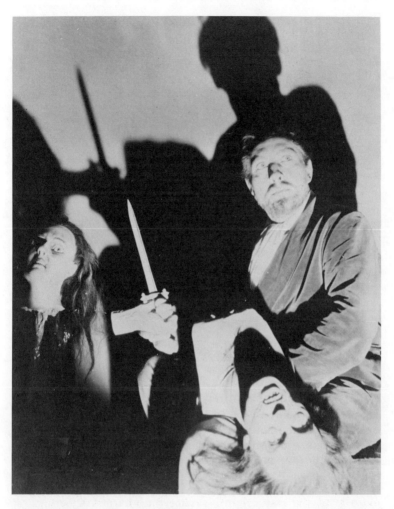

Mystery of the Wax Museum: Lionel Atwill in a grisly publicity shot.

monster on the prowl.   Visiting Atwill's museum with friend
Fay Wray (who is dating one of Atwill's assistants), Farrell
notices that one of the exhibits looks uncannily like a young
suicide victim whose body had been stolen from the morgue.
It is then she begins to suspect the truth behind the exhibits.

Mystery of the Wax Museum: Claude King (left) and Holmes
Herbert watch as Lionel Atwill exhibits one of his sculptures.

Unfortunately, Fay Wray just happens to be an exact
double for a beloved sculpture of Marie Antoinette that had
been destroyed when Atwill's first wax museum burned.
Naturally, she eventually falls into Atwill's clutches and,
striking his face in an attempt to escape, exposes the monster as she shatters what is really a wax mask.   Atwill plans
to add the hapless Fay Wray to his exhibits, but the police
close in at the last minute, saving the girl and shooting
Atwill, who plunges to his death into a vat of his own molten
wax.

Like Doctor X, Mystery of the Wax Museum is a stylish,
strikingly expressionistic thriller, filmed in Technicolor.
Also like its predecessor, the film does not take itself too
seriously, relying heavily for comedic relief on the considerable talents of the snappy Glenda Farrell.

But the picture was not very well received on its initial

release, perhaps because the horror fad was passing out of vogue (although King Kong, also with Fay Wray, would revive the genre's momentum when released in March of 1933), and perhaps because audiences and critics felt somewhat let down by the flawed script; too many unimportant subplots and characters weigh down the narrative.

Fay Wray, playing a more important role in Doctor X, received second billing in both films, and, in Mystery, appears to have been included only as an exceedingly attractive victim for Atwill. The film might have been improved had Miss Wray portrayed Glenda Farrell's role (or vice versa), thereby eliminating one excessive character. But this remedy, too, perhaps would have failed; Fay Wray's screen persona was a bit too passive for aggressive roles (when she attempted a girl-reporter part in a 1938 Universal "B" called The Jury's Secret, it didn't quite work)--also, it is hard to imagine the brassy Glenda Farrell posing as Marie Antoinette.

Mystery of the Wax Museum disappeared from public view shortly after its first release, receiving only very limited reissue screenings throughout the '40s and early '50s. In the late '50s, when the backlog of Warner Bros. features was purchased by United Artists for television and non-theatrical distribution, Mystery of the Wax Museum was not among them. The original 35mm nitrate source materials in the Warners vaults had decomposed, and no print was known to exist. The picture was believed irretrievably lost until, in 1970, a slightly worn but complete print was discovered and screened. Unfortunately, during the film's long absence, historians and fans had built up the movie's reputation too generously. It had come to be regarded as a great lost classic, a flawless masterpiece of the '30s. Of course, on rediscovery, Mystery of the Wax Museum did not live up to its inflated reputation (to be fair, few movies can), and, because of the heightened expectations it aroused, the film seemed that much more disappointing.

Today, seen in a more reasonable light, Mystery of the Wax Museum is highly enjoyable and satisfying on its own terms. In contrast to the more violently explicit, and far less artistic, horror films of recent years, it can justifiably be classified (with similar pictures) as a minor classic.

Mystery of the Wax Museum was remade in 1953 as the

Jimmy the Gent: Bette Davis and James Cagney.

3-D film House of Wax; the basic premise has inspired count-
less (but far less effective) spin-offs and imitations.

•   •   •

Mystery of the Wax Museum was followed by The Keyhole
(105), a private-eye drama with Kay Francis; Private Detective 62 (106), in which William Powell stars as a detective
who falls in love with a woman (Margaret Lindsay) he is investigating (this film is distributed to television under the
title Man Killer); and, Goodbye Again (107), a comedy about
an author (Warren William) who falls in love again with an
old flame and suffers his secretary's efforts to intervene.

Next up was The Kennel Murder Case (108), featuring
William Powell as novelist S. S. Van Dine's debonair sleuth
Philo Vance. Powell had starred as Vance (with Eugene
Pallette as his comic foil, Sergeant Heath) in three mysteries
for Paramount, (The Canary Murder Case, The Greene

Murder Case, and The Benson Murder Case); Basil Rathbone
had portrayed the character in an MGM outing titled The
Bishop Murder Case. Curtiz' The Kennel Murder Case marked
Powell's return to the role ("William Powell returns as Philo
Vance," announce the opening credits); the film is easily
the best of the series.

The unavoidably awkward and stilted Paramount Vance
pictures had been shot during the early sound period (one of
them, The Canary Murder Case was, in fact, shot as a silent
and hastily revamped as a talkie). The Kennel Murder Case
not only benefits from the more assured production techniques
of the early '30s, but from Curtiz' imaginative and highly ef-
ficient direction. While many mysteries of the period still
told their stories at a leisurely pace, Curtiz kept his narrative
moving at lightning speed (the film is a brisk 73 minutes).
Curtiz' enthusiasm aside, Powell's effortless charm carries the
picture (none of the actors who followed him matched his interpretation of the character). Both the star and the director
make The Kennel Murder Case one of the best murder mysteries of the '30s, or of any decade for that matter.

The Kennel Murder Case was followed by Female (109),
a love story with Ruth Chatterton and George Brent;
Mandalay (110), a Kay Francis melodrama; Jimmy the Gent
(111), an exceptionally good comedy--with James Cagney and
Bette Davis--that sought to modify Cagney's gangster image;
The Key, a drama with William Powell, which focuses on the
Irish troubles; and, British Agent (113), a World War I story
with Leslie Howard and Kay Francis.

Black Fury (114), released in 1935, is another Warners
social drama (in the tradition of I am a Fugitive from a Chain
Gang). Paul Muni is cast as a miner used by a gang of
strike breakers to disrupt a union. Muni made an impression,
as always, but he reportedly clashed with Curtiz during
shooting because the director expressed disdain for Muni's
theatrical acting techniques.

The Case of the Curious Bride (115) is a Perry Mason
murder mystery, starring Warren William as Erle Stanley
Gardner's famed attorney. The film, laced with excessive
comedic relief, is less impressive for its own qualities than
for the presence, far down the cast list, of Errol Flynn--then
an up-and-coming actor who played a corpse in one scene.

Front Page Woman (116) is another newspaper story, in which
Bette Davis stars as a girl-reporter. Little Big Shot (117),
is a minor crime drama featuring Sybil Jason, Warners' short-
lived answer to Shirley Temple. This misfire was followed by
Curtiz' first great swashbuckler.

Captain Blood (118)

It is important to pause for a moment and consider the rise
of one Errol Thomson Flynn. Of all actors, it was Flynn who
thrust Michael Curtiz to the top of the studio's director heap.

On the heels of an adventure-filled early life that included being arrested not only for murder but for reputed
slave trading, Flynn drifted into limited work on the London
stage. He was spotted by a Warner Bros. talent agent and
signed to a six-month standard contract. The signing led
Flynn to Hollywood, where he played small parts in two minor
films. Then the famous Flynn luck revealed itself.

The box-office success of The Count of Monte Cristo
had restimulated Hollywood's interest in the lavish costume
epics, which had been such a staple during the silent era.
Every studio clamored for a piece of the action, and Warner
Bros. was no exception. While dusting off the vaults, someone found out that the studio owned the screen rights to
several of Rafael Sabatini's period adventure novels. Captain
Blood was selected for production, and Jack Warner sought
to sign Robert Donat for the lead role. Robert Donat, in
frail health, dropped out at the last minute. A leading man
was needed fast. Who could carry the load? Errol Flynn,
someone suggested. Even today, no one is certain who gave
the go-ahead to star an unknown in a major feature. Hal
Wallis, Mervyn LeRoy--even Michael Curtiz--claimed credit.
Flynn named Jack Warner as the gambler willing to shoulder
the risk. No matter who made the decision, the gamble paid
off, and Errol Flynn became a Hollywood overnight success.

To this point, Curtiz had been the workhorse of the
lot. Astoundingly, in 1933 alone, he had directed seven
features! The man had touched base with every popular
genre of the time--mystery, horror, crime, drama--but had
yet to be acclaimed for work in any one of them. Then just

Captain Blood: Olivia de Havilland with Errol Flynn.

as Errol Flynn had walked into his lucky strike, so did
Michael Curtiz.

Swashbuckling action films--true <u>movies</u> in the literal
sense of the word--swept across the screen under his guidance. Great masses of fighting men crammed together in
violent action and leapt out of each frame in exhilarating bursts
of frenetic energy. No fairy tale fantasy here--actual hack-
ing gore. Curtiz understood the character of men--pirates,
soldiers, gunfighters--in battle. Their code was simple:
kill or be killed. The artist Curtiz had finally found his
canvas.

Unjustly convicted of treason, Dr. Peter Blood (Flynn)
is sold into slavery in Jamaica. He gains the governor's
favor through his medical skills and courts Arabella Bishop
(de Havilland), the niece of his owner, Colonel Bishop
(Atwill).

Captain Blood: Olivia de Havilland and Errol Flynn.

   Curtiz handles the opening scenes in a static manner.
Some of his favorite techniques are evident--shadows play
across walls, and the king's court is lit like an execution
pit. Flynn is quietly restrained, projecting a sharp mixture
of charm and romantic fervor. Olivia de Havilland, barely
20 but with a couple of films already under her belt, teams
perfectly with Flynn. Captain Blood was the first of eight
features she, so ideally, would appear in with the flamboyant
actor.

   Spanish privateers attack Port Royal, and Blood leads
his fellow slaves in a daring escape. Men without countries,
they follow Blood into freedom and become pirates on the
high seas. The shipping lanes ring with Blood's name as
the loot pours in. He enters an ill-advised partnership with
fellow pirate Captain Levasseur (Rathbone) and is forced into
a death duel with his partner over the captured Arabella.

   Shot on location in failing light, Flynn and Rathbone's
duel to the death shows Curtiz at his finest. The two

rivals circle, each testing the other. As the horrified
Arabella watches, the battle rages from one edge of the beach
to the surf. Perfectly timed, Blood runs Lavasseur through,
and Lavasseur falls dead into the face of an oncoming wave.
Honor is satisfied, and Arabella becomes Blood's property.

Lord Willoughby (Henry Stephenson) is also part of the
spoils. He informs Blood that England is at war with Spain
and offers the pirate and his crew royal commissions in the
king's navy. Willoughby is ridiculed until he reveals that
the offer comes from good King William, not the ousted King
James. Blood reclaims England as his home and asks his men
to do the same.

Port Royal is under attack by two French gunboats and
only the pirate ship is on hand to defend the city. The
joyous free Englishmen sail into the fray, eager to crush
their French foes. A furious sea battle ensues as the ships
circle and fire broadside. One French vessel, blasted to
bits when a cannonball finds the powder room, is literally
blown out of the water in a magnificent shot. The second
ship closes in on the pirates. In quick order the privateer
is crippled and sinking.

Blood calls his men to arms, ready to board their foe's
vessel. In a vigorous surge of action, the pirates swing
over to the French deck and the two forces clash for pos-
session of the last seaworthy craft. The fight is swiftly cut
and brutal. Curtiz sweeps his camera in among the swirling
masses of desperate men. The outcome is in doubt even
when the scene cuts to a shot of defeated prisoners sur-
rendering their arms. Which side has prevailed? Lord Willoughby reveals that Blood's men have indeed won out. By
the king's decree, Willoughby dumps the absent Colonel
Bishop as governor and appoints Peter Blood in his place.
The movie ends as Arabella and Peter, in love at last, greet
her flabbergasted uncle in Governor Blood's office.

Captain Blood stands as one of Michael Curtiz's finest
accomplishments. The director keeps the two-hour feature
moving at a brisk pace. Despite the extensive use of
miniatures and great chunks of stock footage worked in from
the 1924 Sea Hawk, each sequence leads to the next in a
smooth flow. The finished product is a fine mix of the

director's European style and his developing American "short-hand."

Curtiz guides Flynn through his star debut without any of the strain that is evident in their later collaborations. Barely 25, Flynn throws sparks as the dashing Sabatino hero. This romantic image sets the pattern for his most remembered roles.

Supposedly, the studio scrapped the first two weeks of finished footage because Flynn hadn't found his acting legs yet. Olivia de Havilland, Basil Rathbone, Guy Kibbee, Henry Stephenson and Robert Barrat all lent solid support to the young actor.

A finely detailed romantic adventure with fresh faces and a dynamic approach, Captain Blood was a box-office hit. Flynn became a star, and Michael Curtiz became the studio's star director. Ahead, for each man, lay several years of professional success.

The stock footage that was used in Captain Blood to expand the scope of the limited budget was lifted from two films--the silent Captain Blood, directed by David Smith and released in 1923, and the 1924 version of The Sea Hawk. Erich Wolfgang Korngold wrote his first movie score for Curtiz' picture; he was the first composer of international repute to be contracted by a Hollywood studio.

The Walking Dead (120)

Captain Blood was followed by Stolen Holiday (119)--another Kay Francis vehicle--and The Walking Dead (120) (Curtiz' last horror film) with Boris Karloff. The horror film boom that had been initiated, in 1931, by Universal's Dracula and Frankenstein was fading by 1936, when The Walking Dead was released. The movie, coming as it did at the end of a cycle, is surprisingly well done.

The story concerns an ex-con musician (Karloff) who is framed (by a crooked lawyer--Ricardo Cortez--and his gang) for the murder of the judge who convicted him. Karloff is convicted and executed in the electric chair (in a fine, shadowy sequence). But the plan goes awry for Cortez

The Walking Dead: Boris Karloff (right) advances on thug Joe Sawyer.

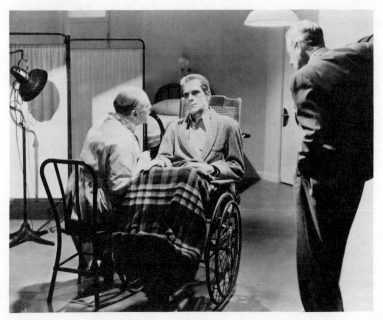

The Walking Dead: Edmund Gwenn (left) and Boris Karloff.

and his minions when Karloff is restored to shuffling life by
scientist Edmund Gwenn, and he seeks revenge on those
responsible for his death. The only problem with this brief
(66 minutes), unpretentious, and very entertaining film is
the contrived manner in which Karloff's revenge is exacted.
In order to maintain audience sympathy for the character,
Karloff never actually murders his victims (though he most
certainly would be justified in doing so).

Unintentionally, he frightens the various gang members
into falling out of windows or into stumbling into the paths
of speeding trains (each death followed by an emotional close-
up of Karloff's face), thereby relieving Karloff of any respon-
sibility for the killings. This flaw certainly lessens the
film's credibility, but Curtiz' direction, Karloff's touching,
restrained performance, and some good and slimy villainy
from Ricardo Cortez and Barton MacLane (in combination with
Hal Mohr's brooding photography) more than compensate.

The Charge of the Light Brigade (121)

Errol Flynn's meteoric rise to stardom caught Warner Bros.
scenarists by surprise. Appropriate vehicles for the young
sensation had to be found quickly, and there was a quick
shuffle of backlog screen treatments. Somewhere, an original script surfaced which examined the events leading up to
the celebrated Charge of the Light Brigade at Balaclava
during the Crimean War. The script--based upon hours of
meticulous historical research, and overflowing with facts--
was clearly unacceptable. This was Hollywood after all, and
Flynn's character had to be shown as the dramatic focal
point of the film. So writers Michael Jacoby and Rowland
Leigh set about revising history. A completely fictitious
groundwork was laid, and elements of old-guard honor, gallantry, and revenge fleshed out the story. The only abso-
lute truth remaining after revision was the fact that the
charge actually did take place!

Because Captain Blood had been such a success, Producer Hal Wallis, clearly, had only one choice for director--
Michael Curtiz. Also on hand was Sol Polito. One of the
best directors of photography in Hollywood, Polito graced
many Warner Bros. releases with his sharp black-and-white
images. He, along with Tony Gaudio, set the tone for the

The Charge of the Light Brigade: Patrick Knowles (left),
Olivia de Havilland, and Errol Flynn pose for a rather stiff
publicity shot.

studio's golden age. Always experimenting with texture,
sheen, and imaginative angles, both cameramen complemented
the Curtiz style.

Max Steiner provided the score for Charge, which was
his first assignment at the studio. Steiner came to Warners
after producing music for some memorable RKO releases, including the score for King Kong. His tenure with Warners
spanned four decades, and his music pumped life into each
feature he worked on.

The storybook structure placed some plot restrictions
on Curtiz. His central character was forced to carry the
load, a challenge Errol Flynn was not yet ready to tackle.
The result is an uneven picture, punctuated by long
stretches of dialogue.

The Charge of the Light Brigade: The climactic charge.

The Charge of the Light Brigade: Patrick Knowles (left),
Nigel Bruce, and Errol Flynn.

Major Geoffrey Vickers (Flynn) of the British 27th
Lancers saves the life of Indian chieftain Surat Khan (C.
Henry Gordon). Any gratitude Khan feels does not prevent
him from entering into a secret alliance with Russia. Using
Russian money and guns, Khan schemes to unite all India
against the British.

Vickers is ordered to buy up every available cavalry
mount; then he sets off for Arabia. The scene shifts to
Calcutta, where Vickers' fiancée, Elsa (Olivia de Havilland),
and his brother, Captain Perry Vickers (Patrick Knowles),
agonize over their new-found love for each other, which they
decide to keep secret from Geoffrey because Elsa feels she
must remain faithful to him.

Curtiz handles the stilted material in a barely workmanlike style. The love triangle, however unrealistic, adds
some underlying tension to the proceedings, but most of the
presentation is unconvincing. Olivia de Havilland's Elsa is
far too sweet, and Patrick Knowles' Captain Vickers is far
too stiff. Flynn plays his early scenes as if he's still trying
to see the mark on the floor he's supposed to stand on. The
only real success during the first third of the feature is a
nicely staged hunt. Native beaters hack through a claustrophobic jungle, driving the frightened prey towards the
hunters. The editing captures the feel of urgency.

Surat Khan begins his revolt, and circumstances lead
his army to the 27th Lancers' home base at Chukote. In an
exciting siege, his forces decimate the defenders, then call
for unconditional surrender. Thinking to save the lives of
helpless women and children, Colonel Campbell (Donald Crisp)
reluctantly submits. He leads his unarmed party into the
teeth of a prearranged trap. The Khan's men fire at will,
sparing no one. Surat Khan allows Major Vickers and Elsa
to escape, canceling his debt. The remnant of the Brigade
is transferred to the Crimea and reassigned to the Light
Brigade. The horror of Chukote is left behind, but the cry
for vengeance echos in Vickers' mind.

Elsa and Perry finally reveal the truth to Geoffrey.
Crushed, betrayed, he turns to his duties for solace; none
is forthcoming. Learning that Surat Khan has fled India
and is on the field with the Russians, Vickers proposes a

frontal assault. His superiors protest that a frontal assault
on entrenched cannon positions would be disastrous.

Once again, honor demands the Khan's death. Vickers
forges orders and joins the Light Brigade for the attack. He
sends his brother back to the commander-in-chief with word
of what he's done. Horrified, the British scramble to support
the advancing cavalry, but they are too late. The Light
Brigade rides into the "valley of death."

Curtiz and second-unit director B. Reeves Eason pulled
out all stops in depicting the charge. With the superimposed
lines of Tennyson's poem flashing across the screen, hundreds
of men and horses move toward the Russian guns. Wave
after wave surge forward, Vickers at the forefront. The Russians, amazed at this tactical blunder, open fire. Unbroken,
the Light Brigade advances, and the valley explodes in fren-
zied turmoil. Explosions scatter men, dirt, and horses in all
directions, yet the advance turns into a full-scale charge.
By sheer force of determination, the Light Brigade smashes
the Russian defenses and turns the tide of the campaign.
Major Vickers dies in the attack, but not before he kills
Surat Khan.

In terms of pace, imagery, and editing, the charge
stands as one of the most remarkable sequences in Hollywood
history. Punctuated by Steiner's score and edited into an
accelerating pace, the overall effect becomes a dizzying succession of jarring images: men fall, horses bolt in terror,
explosions toss clouds of dirt into the air. Masses of fallen
men and broken swords fill the frame in disarray. Above
all this streams the tattered Union Jack. British gallantry
has triumphed again.

The Charge of the Light Brigade was another smash
hit for Flynn as well as for Curtiz. While the finished film
lags overall, Curtiz' execution of sweeping action was superlative. Depression-era audiences responded enthusiastically
to the fictionalized heroics. Most probably, they went home
believing they had learned the "inside" story behind the
Balaclava imbroglio.

There was a silent version of The Charge of the Light
Brigade, a simplistic treatment running only about ten
minutes, released in 1912. The British feature Balaclava

(1930) also used the charge as a plot device.   Curtiz' film
was budgeted at approximately $1,200,000.

Kid Galahad (122)

By 1937, both Michael Curtiz and Bette Davis were stars in
ascension at Warners.   Davis had an Academy Award under
her belt and was about to break out of the studio's assembly-
line production system.   Within four years, she would gain
concessions from Jack Warner which, previously, had been
reserved for his '30s and '40s top stars: script approval,
"A" features built around a star's talents, even director approval.   Kid Galahad would be Davis' fifth film with Curtiz,
and it's interesting to note that she would make only one
more picture with the director (Elizabeth & Essex, 1939).
Apparently, Miss Davis felt (as did many top Warners
stars) that working with Michael Curtiz was a task unequal
to its reward.

Executive producer Hal Wallis assigned Curtiz to
direct a Seaton Miller script.   Also on hand was ace cameraman Tony Gaudio; Max Steiner contributed part of the musical score.   The production unit was complemented by the cast.
Leads Edward G. Robinson and Davis were supported by Harry
Carey (in a fine performance) and Jane Bryan.   Warners
stock company players, Ben Weldon, Joseph Crehan and
Frank Faylen, rounded out the cast.   Wayne Morris, a young
actor being groomed as star material, played the title role
of boxer Kid Galahad.   Morris was barely competent on-
screen, but he was to gain "star" rank as a fighter pilot
during World War II and was probably the only Hollywood
star to attain "Ace" status during the war.

Humphrey Bogart had a featured role as Robinson's
main rival, "Turkey" Morgan.   Playing the "stock gangster"
had earned him his studio contract in The Petrified Forest.   In
Kid Galahad Bogart worked under Curtiz for the first time.

Kid Galahad was dated by the time the picture was
released.   An unknown fighter (Morris), under manager Nick
Donati (Robinson), starts a storybook climb to the top of the
"ring world."   At heart a gentlemanly type, Nick's longtime
girlfriend Fluff (Davis) names the boxer Kid Galahad.   Love
disrupts the training camp when Donati's young sister Marie

(Bryan) falls for the Kid. Even hard-bitten Fluff is at-
tracted to the change-of-pace fighter. Jealous and angered,
Nick arranges a championship bout with rival manager Morgan
(Bogart). It's a fight the inexperienced Kid can't win, and
Nick guarantees Morgan that he himself will be betting against
his own fighter. Indeed, because Nick spitefully gives his
boxer all the wrong guidance, the fight goes heavily against
the Kid for several rounds. He takes a terrific beating until
Fluff and Marie finally convince Nick that the Kid never
double-crossed him. Nick has the Kid change tactics, and
Galahad battles his way to the title.

Morgan loses a fortune. Vengeful, he shoots it out
with Nick, and both are killed. Nick's influence ends, and
the Kid and Marie are free to marry. Only Fluff is the
loser.

Curtiz' direction transcends the breezy script. He
gives each lead a special feel to carry across. Robinson im-
bues his character with barely concealed anger. Alternately
lovable and deceitful, his Nick Donati is especially noteworthy.
Bette Davis plays the long-suffering Fluff with such innate
wisdom that the viewer is led to expect a happy ending. In
the picture, Bogart becomes a cold, malevolent hood; Curtiz
must have admired his performance.

The fight scenes were handled in a crisp, fast style.
Harshly lit and fast-cut in the typical Warners pace, the
boxing sequences enhance the film as well as advance it.
Hailed upon its release as a fine, rousing fight picture, Kid
Galahad stands as an excellent example of the Warner Bros.
talent pool--and the film kept Curtiz on a winning streak.

•   •   •

Kid Galahad was followed by Mountain Justice (123), a minor
drama with Josephine Hutchinson.

The Perfect Specimen (124)

Comedy and Michael Curtiz did not mix well, and it's not
surprising. Apparently a cold, sardonic man, Curtiz never
seemed to get a handle on his few light entertainment assignments. He was always a master of sweeping action, solid

characterization, and powerful dramatic interplay, so his
style was more suited to side-of-the-mouth sarcasm than to
frilly drawing-room humor.

With The Perfect Specimen, Curtiz faced the additional
liability of having Errol Flynn in the lead. Still developing
as an actor, Flynn had his limitations. Specimen was his
first comedy role and, despite his natural screen charm, he
seems just as uneasy with the subject as the director does.

Fortunately, the Warner Bros. stock company was able
to help smooth things over. Joan Blondell co-starred in the
picture, and accomplished comedy pros Edward Everett
Horton, Hugh Herbert, and Allen Jenkins provided solid
support for Flynn.

The perfect specimen is Gerald Beresford Wicks (Flynn),
heir of a wealthy family. Raised by his Aunt Leona (May
Robson) to embody the Spartan ethic of "a sound mind in a
healthy body," Wicks has been kept completely removed from
outside human contact. As a result, the young man is so
intellectually smart that he is socially stupid.

Enter newspaper woman Mona Carter (Blondell), who
smashes into the Wicks' estate and disrupts the entire setup.
In short order, she draws the perfect specimen out into an
imperfect world. With Mona's help and the genuine curios-
ity of a child to stir him, Gerald progresses from a wide-eyed
innocent to a fully mature man. Nature takes its course, and
Gerald and Mona fall in love.

Seen rarely today, The Perfect Specimen was an excellent star vehicle for Errol Flynn. In it, he was able to
parody the natural attributes that elevated him to stardom.
Curtiz held the material together at a lax pace, unable to
take advantage of most of the comedic opportunities. The
film was a success by the sheer force of Flynn's box-office
appeal, and it would be awhile before either he or Curtiz
would be assigned to another comedy.

●   ●   ●

Gold Is Where You Find It (125), a western drama pitting
gold miners against ranchers, was shot in lush Technicolor.
Starring George Brent and Olivia de Havilland, with the

The Adventures of Robin Hood: (from left) Olivia de Havilland, Errol Flynn, Eugene Pallette, and Basil Rathbone enjoy
a feast in Sherwood Forest.

usual outstanding support from Claude Rains, the film was
expensively mounted as a showcase for Technicolor (unfortunately, the picture is often seen on television today in a
black-and-white version), and it was Curtiz' successful handling of this picture that led to his second and most famous
Errol Flynn swashbuckler.

The Adventures of Robin Hood (126)

Released in 1938, The Adventures of Robin Hood is arguably
Curtiz' finest swashbuckler. There are those who prefer
The Sea Hawk for its extensive historical detail and emotionally deeper performances, but The Adventures of Robin Hood,
shot in brilliant Technicolor, is by far the more popular and
entertaining of the two films. Everything is so right, from
the impressive sets and costumes to the appropriately simplistic acting (and "simplistic" acting, in a film of mythic stature

The Adventures of Robin Hood: Errol Flynn (right) challenges Basil Rathbone in the climactic duel.

like this, should not be interpreted as a flaw by any means),
that it is somewhat jarring to realize that Curtiz almost didn't
direct the picture.

During their previous films together, Errol Flynn had
acquired an intense dislike for Curtiz, who frequently

disparaged Flynn's acting abilities, and the swashbuckler had
been lobbying with the Warners brass in an effort to dis-
associate himself from the director.

When production of The Adventures of Robin Hood began, William Keighley was, in accordance with Flynn's wishes,
at the helm, directing. But shooting immediately fell behind
schedule, and Keighley's rushes were so lighthearted and
leisurely paced that Jack Warner was displeased. Overriding
Flynn's objections, he dismissed Keighley and replaced him
with Curtiz (although Keighley shot only a small amount of
the footage included in the release print, he did receive a
co-director credit, probably for contractual reasons). Under
Curtiz' whip-cracking command, production picked up immediately, and the eventual results more than justified Jack
Warner's decision. Flynn may not have cared for Curtiz per-
sonally, but he certainly couldn't--and to his credit didn't--
deny the man's directorial prowess.

The film is a virile, colorful, romantic fairytale enhanced
by a rousing Korngold score--the production difficult to fault
on any level. Perhaps the gaiety of the performers is a bit
forced at times (the cast seems to spend a great deal of time
laughing), and the comedic relief supplied by Herbert Mundin
is excessive on occasion, but it seems like quibbling to criti-
cize such an otherwise flawless picture. The cast--Flynn, the
beautiful Olivia de Havilland, Basil Rathbone, Claude Rains,
Alan Hale, and Patrick Knowles--are all in peak form. A
smash hit with the critics and public, extremely successful in
reissues, and one of the most widely seen films on television,
The Adventures of Robin Hood can have little that is new
said about it. This vastly entertaining film is, simply, one
of the most popular movies ever made--a permanent classic,
and deserving of such respect.

There had been previous silent versions of the Robin
Hood legend filmed before Curtiz' production: Robin Hood,
a one-reel version released by Kalem in 1908; Robin Hood and
His Merry Men, a one-reel British production released by
Clarendon in 1908; a version from Eclair in 1912; another
British version in 1913, titled In the Days of Robin Hood; a
version produced by Thanhouser in 1913, titled Robin Hood;
and, of course, the legendary Douglas Fairbanks production
Robin Hood, released in 1922.

The Adventures of Robin Hood: Olivia de Havilland with
Errol Flynn.

The final negative cost on Curtiz' The Adventures of
Robin Hood was approximately $1,900,000. The film was re-
issued in 1948 to huge public response, reissued once more
in black-and-white, and remains today, with Curtiz' other
masterpieces (Casablanca and the original King Kong), one
of the most popular movies distributed to television.

•   •   •

Four's a Crowd: Olivia de Havilland with Errol Flynn.

The versatile Curtiz followed The Adventures of Robin Hood
with Four Daughters (127), a small-town soap opera that
was tremendously successful with the critics and the public.
Starring Claude Rains and, as his daughters, the Lane
Sisters (Rosemary, Lola, and Priscilla), the film is a
touching, nicely acted, and believable account of small-town
life. John Garfield is excellent in his first movie role.
Four Daughters was such a hit that it led to three sequels,
two of which were directed by Curtiz.

Four's a Crowd (128) came next. The film gave Errol
Flynn and Olivia de Havilland a chance to attempt light
comedy, and they succeeded quite well in this romantic
farce.

Angels with Dirty Faces (129)

Angels with Dirty Faces was the first Cagney/Curtiz team-up

in several years. Both men had matured in terms
of style and technique, each firmly establishing his own
strengths and screen personality. Cagney's popularity had
grown to such an extent that, after breaking away from
Warners for a couple of years, he'd been allowed to return
when the new studio (Grand National) he had signed with
collapsed. He came back with a big contract and began
work on a stretch of his best features. Curtiz, of course,
had stayed on the assembly line. By 1938, he was clearly
the top director on the lot.

Warner Bros. had always led the way in producing
hardhitting gangster pictures. From Little Caesar (1930)
and Public Enemy (1931) through Marked Woman (1937),
most of the major stars on the studio payroll had appeared
in the popular box-office draws. Even though the cycle
had run its course, the public wanted to see Cagney in the
type of role that had made him a star. The "Dead-End"
Kids were also under contract at Warners. After a smash
debut with Humphrey Bogart in Goldwyn's Dead-End (1937),
they signed on to appear in a series of B's as well as in
some major productions, so it seemed only natural to work
them into the new Cagney feature. Perennial Cagney co-star
Pat O'Brien was on hand, as well as a full-blown stock company cast: Humphrey Bogart, Ann Sheridan, and George
Bancroft. Sol Polito handled the cameras, and Max Steiner
composed a stirring score.

The film traces the rise, fall, and redemption of gangster Rocky Sullivan. Virtually a one-man gang, Rocky is
released from jail and returns to his old neighborhood, seeking old friends and his erstwhile partner, lawyer James
Frazier (Bogart). In short order he is rolled by a teenaged
gang (The Dead-End Kids). Then he runs into a childhood
sweetheart, Laury (Sheridan), and visits his lifelong pal,
Father Jerry Connelly (O'Brien). The priest welcomes Rocky
back, but chides him for becoming the idol of the neighborhood kids. Rocky laughs off the priest's scolding and heads
for the nightclub that Frazier has opened with money Rocky
had gone to jail for stealing. Frazier is flustered. He
stalls Rocky and plots with mob-boss MacKeefer (Bancroft)
to put the intruder out of the way permanently.

Curtiz moved the film along at a lively pace, brisk even
for him. Rocky barges into scenes (even at Father Connelly's

Angels with Dirty Faces: Pat O'Brien (second from right)
leads James Cagney (on O'Brien's left) down the "last mile."
This production photo reveals the sparse economy of the
set, which Curtiz effectively disguised in the film itself
through the use of tighter shots, oblique angles, and atmos-
pheric lighting.

church) and turns events to his favor.   Cagney, on-screen
throughout, orchestrates his performance like a virtuoso
conductor.   His Rocky Sullivan is a pusher, a mover, and a
shaker, who lives by a surprisingly honorable code.

Frazier violates that code.   He and MacKeefer move
against Rocky, first legally, then physically.   They fail.
Rocky sidesteps the legal trap and turns the tables on the
villains' gunmen.   In a tense scene, Rocky confronts his ex-
partner and guns both him and mob-boss MacKeefer down.
This sets the stage for a violent warehouse siege.   Rocky,
who is cornered, holds off the police until Father Connelly
arrives.   The priest convinces the police to hold their fire,
and he enters the warehouse.   Rocky takes the priest
hostage and attempts to escape.   He fails, and is captured.

The warehouse battle is a nicely staged segment.
Cagney rushes from window to window, firing at police and
dodging machine-gun bullets. Tear gas spreads through the
building, and the gasping criminal grows more desperate.

Quickly tried, then sentenced to die in the electric
chair, the stoic Rocky clings to his code; he's been caught,
so there's no sense crying about it. Father Connelly begs
Rocky to break down, to be afraid of dying, so that some
of the kids who idolize him might not follow in his footsteps.
Outraged, Rocky refuses. To die like that would violate
the code he's lived by. He marches down Death Row. But
when officials start to strap him into the chair, he breaks
down. Rocky Sullivan, big-time hood, dies sobbing for his
life. The Dead-End Kids, shaken, follow Father Connelly
back to church.

Even today, people speculate whether Rocky Sullivan
turned "yellow" at the last moment. The truth is left unre-
solved. Cagney gives no hint in his performance; O'Brien
doesn't either. Curtiz handles the tension-charged scene
straight, injecting it with no romanticism. Rocky cries,
screams, begs, and tries to claw his way out of his predica-
ment. His choking voice is finally cut off by the hum of
the electric generator. The emotionally charged scene provides an image that lingers, long after the feature has
ended.

Critics hailed the film, especially Cagney's performance.
Audiences loved it, and the feature did almost twice the
business of any previous Cagney release. Michael Curtiz
moved on to his next assignment--there was more work to
attend to.

Dodge City (130)

By 1939, Hollywood studios were showing renewed interest in
a genre--the western--that had grown stale through willful
neglect. Once a reliable box-office draw, westerns had, by
1935, declined in prestige at the major studios. The few
still being produced were either cheap serials or assembly-
line "B" pictures featuring an endless parade of has-beens
and unknown newcomers. Studio publicity departments ran
the gamut in their attempts to restore the gleam to shopworn

goods, but the ticket buyers stayed away. The tastes of
Depression-era moviegoers had changed, and the western
was just one of several genres to fall out of favor with the
public.

Striking out in "new" directions to acquire bankable
properties, Hollywood did then as it does now--fed on its
own past. Just as another well-worn genre, the gangster
film, had been rejuvenated through the injection of tougher,
more explicit violence, the tired western was pumped full of
new life, too, with higher budgets and more impressive
talent both in front of and behind the camera.

Director Fritz Lang bought Teutonic fury to the legend
of the James brothers in The Return of Frank James (1940).
The year before, John Ford had adapted a magazine story
("The Stage to Lordsberg"), for the screen, retitling it
Stagecoach and casting in the lead a nine-year western vet
named John Wayne. Jack Warner, never one to let a box-
office dollar slip past him, sent the word out to his production staff: make westerns, not just any westerns--make
solid "A" budget westerns.

The cost-conscious Warner Bros. studio consistently
turned out impressive and energetic first-rate features.
Even low-scale "B" films appeared looking better than their
budget figures would imply; most were competently written,
technically well-mounted, tightly directed, and crisply
edited. The final results never seemed shoddy or cheap,
even though the entire budget for a typical 1939 feature
wouldn't pay for a half-hour network television sitcom today.
An "A" budget at Warners was the exception rather than
the rule. That kind of money brought the studio's topnotch
talent with it, so when Dodge City was chosen in response
to Jack Warner's edict, Curtiz was selected to direct and
handed a cast loaded with star-power and talent.

Errol Flynn, then at the peak of his popularity, headed
the cast, with Olivia de Havilland providing Flynn's romantic
interest (even though the "Oomph Girl," Ann Sheridan was
on hand). The supporting cast comprised familiar Warners
stock company faces: Alan Hale, Frank McHugh, Guinn "Big
Boy" Williams, John Litel, and Ward Bond, with both Victor
Jory and Henry Travers brought in from the freelance ranks.

Dodge City: Errol Flynn and Olivia de Havilland.

Bruce Cabot was cast as Flynn's primary nemesis.
Cabot was the scion of a wealthy family and had entered the
acting field in the early thirties.   The actor's solid good
looks had earned him semileads and top, "heavy" roles in
some excellent features.   In King Kong, he had defied the
giant ape to rescue Fay Wray and, in Fritz Lang's Fury, he
headed the lynch mob that tried to burn Spencer Tracy alive.

Errol Flynn found in Cabot a kindred spirit. Each man was
as much at home in a bar or a brawl--offscreen as well as
on. The two struck up a long friendship that lasted until
the early '50s. At that time, a business venture between
them went sour, and Cabot brought legal action against
Flynn. But in the late '30s, Flynn did his best for his
friends, and due to Flynn's influence at the studio, Cabot
landed the Dodge City role of Jeff Surrett, corrupt city
boss. If Flynn hadn't recommended Cabot for the role, most
likely the part would have been played by a Warners contract actor--possibly Humphrey Bogart or Paul Kelly. With
Cabot in the role, Curtiz and his writers made the two
characters opposing equals; Cabot's Surrett was just as vil-
lainous as Flynn's Hatton was virtuous.

Dodge City opens with a long prologue that introduces
the characters and sets the tone of the film. America is
progressing further westward. Expansion is just a matter
of time, as is having to deal with the Indians. The rail-
roads spearhead the invasion of the plains, and Colonel
Dodge is the visionary who forsees large cities full of happy,
pioneering settlers.

Taking full advantage of his resources, Curtiz brings
to the screen a vast, beautiful prairie through which a
railroad steam engine cuts with majestic bearing. He under-
lines the progress theme as, overland, a stagecoach attempts
to race this "tea-pot on rails." In an exciting and well-
paced blend of crosscuts and back projection, the railroad
engine wins the race and progress is served.

Max Steiner provided a memorable score for Dodge
City, especially for this train race segment, and he assigned
Guinn Williams a short tune that serves to introduce Hatton
(Flynn) and his two pals in the next sequence. As the
train continues onward, Curtiz pulls away from the scene, and
backs up to a bluff, where the three men are arriving.
Williams is singing his ditty, and Flynn is shown for the first
time.

The three men discuss the train race. We learn that,
during the westward expansion, they have been scouting the
area for Colonel Dodge. The prologue ends as the trio moves
on, leaving Dodge City at the mercy of the greedy Cabot and
his murderous henchmen. In one finely crafted sequence,

rancher John Litel argues with Surrett over a cattle payment.
Surrett, in a tight close-up that reveals his insincerity,
tells the doubting cattleman to be at the saloon that night
for the money. Curtiz' camera follows Litel as he dismounts
and moves to the swinging doors of Surrett's saloon; it pans
up and away as he enters. The scene then cuts to the interior, as swarms of cowboys and bargirls crowd around the
gaming tables. On stage performing is Ann Sheridan (obviously in the film only as a box-office draw, since her total
screen time amounts to less than ten minutes). Surrett
greets Litel and leads the cattleman to the bar, excusing
himself to "get the money." As Surrett walks off, the frame
tightens. Cabot approaches henchman Victor Jory. With a
casual head toss from Cabot, Litel's death warrant is signed.
Jory then unsuccessfully attempts to provoke the peaceful
Litel and, finally, shoots the innocent rancher down in "self-
defense."

Flynn's inevitable return to the graft-ridden town is
low-key. A spectacular cattle stampede, caused by Olivia de
Havilland's drunken brother, forms the bridge leading from
Hatton's indifference to his eventual involvement. De
Havilland's brother is killed, creating an icy barrier between
the two would-be lovers, and Hatton must find a way to get
through to her. Although he vows to move on, Hatton's
growing love for Abbie and his hatred of Surrett's amoral
rule are the emotional foundations on which Curtiz builds the
rest of the film.

Up to this point, the brisk pace set by the director
contributes to an overall light tone. The antics of Tex and
Rusty, the lighthearted dialogue of the principals, and the
epic sweep of the story predominate. Utilizing his favorite
technique of blending comedy and drama, Curtiz sets the
next meeting between Hatton and Surrett in a barber shop.
While Alan Hale's Rusty luxuriates in a bath in the back of
the shop, Hatton, for the first time in months, gets a shave.

The barber is talking, telling Hatton of the rancher's
murder. At the mention of Surrett's name, Hatton's eyes
widen, and the camera shifts to the feet of two men entering
the barber shop. The movement is ominous--slow and steady
--and, when the barber stutters nervously, then stops talking, it's apparent that Cabot has just entered.

In a fine three-way cut, Surrett complains about being denied the bath occupied by Rusty, at the same time soapy Hale continues to sing. Flynn, in medium shot, calmly tells Cabot that Rusty is entitled to his fair share of time in the tub. A fast cut to Surrett's face punctuates the scene; his expression changes from anger to recognition. Hale breaks the tension by dashing out of the tub, clutching his pants, and dripping suds.

Alan Hale was a favorite of Curtiz, and the director encouraged the veteran scene stealer toward achieving some of the actor's best work. Whereas a director like Raoul Walsh brought out the good-natured, sentimental aspects of Hale's personality, Curtiz usually exposed the actor's mischievous side. As a result, Hale and Guinn Williams usually wound up looking to Flynn as a father figure who was there to guide them through trouble and to save them when necessary.

In Dodge City, Hale shines as Rusty, a combination boy/man/innocent conniver. The actor lends extra flavor to the scene in which Rusty proclaims himself to be a "new man who done signed the pledge" and is saved from the "sins" of alcohol. There's a cut to the saloon sign, and the camera drifts down to the solitary Hale, who is looking for all the world like a naughty ten-year old caught with his hand in the cookie jar.

While Tex and the other trail hands revel in Surrett's saloon, Hale joins an all-woman temperance group; in no time he is standing before them, pouring out the story of his mighty battle with booze. Surrett's saloon is a hotbed of ex-Union vets, and Tex, of course, is pure Dixie.

In a scene that, by a few years, predates a very similar one in Casablanca, Curtiz again employs one of his favorite motifs. Ann Sheridan leads a bevy of chorus girls in a patriotic song, and most of the Civil War vets join in. Tex, disgusted, calls for his boys to sing Dixie. The camera cuts from group to group as the two songs vie for supremacy in the bar. The outcome is in doubt until Williams spots a regimental picture of Union troops hanging above the bar and disdainfully tosses his beer stein through it. Instantly, a chaotic fight breaks out, as the miniature "War Between the States" becomes a barroom brawl. With his usual flair for action, Curtiz makes the large set seem to overflow with battling figures. Men fly from balconies, crash through windows, shatter chairs over one another's heads, and grapple in tight close-up.

In the midst of all this violent action, Curtiz manages to provide some light touches: as the fight begins, a miner runs out with one of the saloon girls slung over his back; no one is killed even though it seems everyone is trying to kill one another; in one long shot, a table flies across the frame ten feet in the air; and, finally, when the barroom can no longer contain the apocalyptic battle, the crowd smashes through the saloon wall into (where else?) the temperance meeting, where Rusty continues to struggle with his testimony.

Vows are forgotten as Hale leaps into the fray, but his participation is brief. In no time at all, he's staggering across the floor; knocked senseless, he falls, grinning, behind the bar. The battle ends as Tex stands center frame and fires his gun, announcing the South's "victory."

After the fight scene, there is a sharp turn in style. Surrett rages over the damage to his wrecked saloon and, from behind the bar, a groggy Rusty emerges, still babbling his life story. As suddenly as the brawl had broken out, a lynch party is formed. Cabot sees his chance to get even with Flynn by hanging Flynn's friend. The film's tone darkens as Rusty finally realizes what is about to happen.

The mob surges from the bar, bent on murder. Curtiz solemnly handles Hatton's subsequent rescue of Rusty. Hatton faces down Cabot and the mob; the scene is played so straight that a viewer, seeing Hatton draw on Cabot, finds it believable that one man can control an angry mob.

The rescue is successful. Hatton, still intent on moving on, turns down the job of sheriff. Clearly, something has to change his mind, and something does.

A cheerful school outing, supervised by Abbie (Olivia de Havilland), rolls down the main street. Steiner's merry music adds a warm touch to the scene, even as the wagon

loaded with school children heads into the midst of a pitched
gun battle.

Surrett's saloon is the site of a more deadly fight this
time. A group of men dash into the path of the school
wagon. They fire back at the saloon, and the camera
shifts away from the gun battle, over to the frightened
horses. The animals bolt, and Abbie, along with one of the
children, fights to control them. The shackle breaks, the
horses stampede, and the boy gets tangled in the reins and
is dragged alongside the wagon. It is Flynn who finally
stops the horses, but the boy, who turns out to be the son
of murdered rancher John Litel, is dead.

So are Flynn's inhibitions about staying in Dodge City.
Curtiz dissolves from a crumpled paper badge on the dead
boy's chest to a real badge on Flynn's belt. Vowing to
stop the lawlessness, Hatton attacks every aspect of the
town's corruption. In a fast and economical montage, the
new sheriff stops gun fights and lynchings, and he fills the
jail.

Cabot again confronts Flynn, this time attempting to
buy him off. The two men face each other as equals, each
confident he is in the right. Cabot oozes insincerity; Flynn
looks on contemptuously.

His efforts at bribery unsuccessful, Cabot takes a
back seat as the town enjoys a rebirth. New settlers pour
in. The church is packed, and men surrender their guns.
But Surrett refuses to give in. Shortly, the newspaper
editor is killed. Again, it's Victor Jory doing Cabot's
dirty work. (The shooting is actually committed in shadow
form, another of Curtiz' visual trademarks.) The murder
of the likable Joe Clemens (played by Frank McHugh) sets
up the film's conclusion.

Flynn is forced to smuggle prisoner Jory and main
witness Abbie out of town on the same train. Of course,
Cabot and his gang are on board. They trap Flynn and
Hale in the mail car. Guns blaze, and Curtiz isolates each
man as bullets chew up the walls. The outcome is still
uncertain when a fire breaks out and Olivia de Havilland
bursts into the car. A quick series of cuts between her,
Cabot, and Flynn make the villain's intent clear. He grabs

Abbie, forcing Wade and Rusty to surrender. Laughing,
Cabot frees Jory and locks the three others in the burning
car. Outside, the spreading fire forces Surrett and his men
to mount their horses at a full gallop. Rusty, in the meantime, has chopped out the wall of the mail car with a fire
ax. In a contrived finish, Wade and Rusty pick off Cabot
and his men one by one, each of the foes melodramatically
hitting the ground and rolling face up.

The somewhat hurried conclusion ties up loose ends:
Tex and Rusty lament that Dodge City has become too
civilized for them; Wade is happy--he and Abbie have become engaged; and, Colonel Dodge turns up with the story
of an even wilder town. Virginia City, he says, cries out
for a lawman like Flynn. Abbie reluctantly agrees that the
West might need Wade almost as much as she does, and the
entire group, followed by the camera, rides off into the
sunset toward an implied sequel (see Virginia City chapter).

Dodge City represented the Warner Bros. assembly
line at its finest. A tight, fast-paced entertainment, the
movie demanded little of its audience, returned a handsome
profit, and justified Jack Warner's insistence on an "A" budget. However, Dodge City did little to enhance the careers
of any of its principal actors. Flynn's screen image might
actually have been slightly tarnished by his appearance in a
western.

Once the public accepted the formerly dashing cava-
lier in more "Americanized" roles, a lot of his "glitter" disappeared. Indeed, within a few years, Flynn would be
wearing contemporary business suits and attempting light
comedy. Curtiz, in the meantime, having finished Dodge
City, prepared for his next feature.

•   •   •

After Dodge City, Curtiz efficiently dashed off Sons of
Liberty (131), a patriotic Technicolor short subject starring
Claude Rains. This, Curtiz' only film of this type, won an
Academy Award as the Best Short Subject of 1939. The film
was followed by Daughters Courageous (132) (the first sequel to Four Daughters), after which Curtiz prepared for
his next Errol Flynn epic.

The Private Lives of Elizabeth and Essex (133)

Shot in perfect Technicolor and finely crafted, this film is
as lavish as any Warners "A" feature could have been, at
the time. From Bette Davis and Errol Flynn as the title
royalty, right down through Olivia de Havilland, Donald
Crisp, Alan Hale, Henry Daniell, and Vincent Price in support, the film is loaded with promise. The script, based on
the play by Maxwell Anderson, offered a delicately balanced
scenario that attempted to function on several levels. It
was left to Curtiz to make each faction surface.

Following an unexpected military victory, the Earl of
Essex (Flynn) returns to London where a tremendous crowd
turns out to hail him. Rejoicing privately, Queen Elizabeth
(Davis) rebuffs Essex before the court for losing a chance
to capture the Spanish treasure fleet. Furious at what he
believes to be jealousy on the Queen's part, Lord Essex accepts her dismissal and retires to his country castle.

There, he is goaded by friends and political enemies
alike to return to active duty. He resists until the Queen
herself sends word, requesting his services. Once Essex
is back at court, Elizabeth appoints him Master of Ordnance,
a post that will keep him close at hand, yet far from any
opportunity to gain more public stature.

An Irish rebellion led by the Earl of Tyrone (Hale)
provides Lord Essex' enemies with their chance to rid themselves of him. Appealing to his pride, they rap him into
leading an army against Tyrone, then plot to undermine him
while he fights in Ireland. No word is allowed to pass between Essex and Elizabeth, and Essex is pulled down in
defeat because of lack of support. Furious, he gathers a
new army and storms London, surrounding Whitehall Palace
and calling for the Queen's abdication.

Helpless, Elizabeth pretends to comply, and Essex,
still in love with her, disbands his forces. The vengeful
Queen then orders the Earl imprisoned for treason; he is
quickly found guilty.

As the day of execution draws near, the agonized
Queen sends for her prisoner. Her love forces her to offer
him both his life and a throne as royal consort. Still proud,

The Private Lives of Elizabeth and Essex: Errol Flynn in
full regalia.

and realizing that only full power would satisfy him, Essex
rejects her proposal and walks to the execution block,
leaving the lonely Queen to her empty throne room.

        Despite some masterful touches, Curtiz cannot hold
the film together. Although Bette Davis gives a tour de

Four Wives: (from left) Lola Lane, Frank McHugh, Rosemary
Lane, Claude Rains, May Robson, Dick Foran, and Gale Page.

force performance as the "virgin Queen," Errol Flynn is unable to match her histrionics.   Taking direction from a man
he had come to dislike and acting with a woman he despised,
Flynn merely walks through the film.   He appears disinter-
ested in most of his scenes, and is barely able to keep from
laughing as he proclaims unending love for the pinch-faced
Davis.   Only in his final scene, as the two lovers face each
other and proudly accept their fates, does Flynn come alive.
Both are torn between love and power, and though Curtiz
manages to invest an ironic sadness into the climax, the final product rings false.

●   ●   ●

The Private Lives of Elizabeth and Essex was followed by
the second Four Daughters sequel, Four Wives (134), in
which the title characters were married.   (The third sequel,
called, inevitably enough, Four Mothers, was directed by
William Keighley in 1941.)

Virginia City (135)

During the late '30s, Curtiz entered one of his most productive and demanding periods. Alternating between outstanding "A" features and well-produced programmers, the next several years would see him direct films of almost every type: westerns (Virginia City, Santa Fe Trail); swashbucklers (Sea Hawk); psychological melodramas (Sea Wolf); musicals (Yankee Doodle Dandy); even jingoistic propaganda (Mission to Moscow). Such a varied workload makes a letdown understandable, and Virginia City is just such a letdown.

Actually a movie with a story to tell, the film is hard to take at face value. Once again, an unhappy Errol Flynn co-stars with Randolph Scott and Miriam Hopkins in a Civil War drama of gold, conflict, and betrayal.

Kerry Bradford (Flynn), a Union Army officer, escapes a Confederate prison camp commanded by Vance Irby (Scott). Ordered to block a gold shipment intended for the desperate Confederate forces at Richmond, Bradford travels to the western city under cover. Along the way he meets and falls in love with saloon-singer Julia Hayne (Miriam Hopkins). Julia turns out to be a southern spy, as well as an "old friend" of Irby's. Realizing that the newly arrived Bradford could defeat their plans, Irby enlists Julia to trick the Union officer into a trap. Their plan works, and the gold shipment leaves Virginia City under cover of an attack on the Union garrison by outlaw John Murrell (Humphrey Bogart). Captive, Bradford goes with it.

If the film sounds exciting, it isn't. Nothing works. Flynn walks through his scenes, bored, uninterested, totally unconvincing. Of all his films with Curtiz, this is his worst performance. He is especially bad when, during the escape sequence, he confronts Scott. So wide-eyed and waxen is Flynn, it's strange that Curtiz allowed the scene to be printed. The entire blame cannot rest with the actor, however. Miriam Hopkins brings new vistas to the term "miscast." Ostensibly the female lead, she bungles through a very unconvincing musical number and plays some awful "love" scenes with Flynn. Even more embarrassing is Humphrey Bogart as a half-breed bandit. Still casting around the studio for some decent work, he found himself

wearing a pencil-thin mustache and speaking with a cartoon
accent.

Bradford soon finds himself in sympathy with his cap-
tors. When the wagon train is attacked by Marrell's
bandits, Irby is killed and Bradford takes command. The
Union forces tracking the gold shipment arrive in time to
save the southerners, but Bradford has hidden the gold.
He refuses to reveal where it is and is imprisoned, facing
execution until Julia appeals directly to President Lincoln,
who pardons the prisoner. The lovers are reunited, and
the gold will help rebuild the south.

Such hackneyed material required a firm directorial
hand. Curtiz, whether unhappy with Flynn, Hopkins or the
story, just did not provide it. The finished product re-
sembles a Three Stooges short. The film is frenetic, disjointed, and, finally, empty.

The Sea Hawk (136)

In his autobiography, My Wicked, Wicked Ways, Errol Flynn
constantly complained of being pushed into one-dimensional
roles. "Westerns and swashbucklers," he wrote, "were the
ruin of creative personalities." Hollywood had always taken
pains to prove him right. But had Flynn taken some time off
from his usual roistering and focused a sharp look at the
finished cut of The Sea Hawk, even his self-mocking aesthetic
sense might have recognized a terrific movie.

The year 1940 saw the release of only two features
directed by Michael Curtiz--the dreadful Virginia City and
the dazzling film, The Sea Hawk. In fact, from the early
'40s through the end of his Warners contract, the director's
workload would be a much lighter one than he had been used
to. As a result, Curtiz paid greater attention to detail and
characterization in worthwhile projects, and less attention in
minor productions.

The Sea Hawk stands as one of those worthwhile projects. It was put into preproduction after the success of
Captain Blood. Once again the flavor of Rafael Sabatini's
original novel was fleshed out and a Seton Miller screenplay
reworked by Howard Koch. Sol Polito oversaw the black-and-

The Sea Hawk: Errol Flynn (center).

white photography in the film (one of his most successful
productions).   Erich Wolfgang Korngold contributed the lush
score, a fully rounded collection of orchestral bombast.

While fellow Warner Bros. composer Max Steiner's music
added dynamic flavor to action scenes, Korngold's forte was
subtle underscoring.   More restrained and better structured
than Steiner, Korngold added heraldic romanticism to historical epics.   The brass fanfare he used to open the film
warns the audience that some fireworks are in store.

Apparently, Errol Flynn approached his role with some
interest.   Definitely not as inhibited as he had been in
Elizabeth and Essex, or as wooden as he had been in
Virginia City, in The Sea Hawk he turns in a well-defined
performance.   In fact, The Sea Hawk ranks as the best of
all the Flynn/Curtiz collaborations since Robin Hood (co-
directed with William Keighley).   Originally running 126
minutes, the script gave Curtiz ample opportunity to inject

his personal touches. His entire bag of tricks came into play--tilted cameras, sarcastic readings, shadows on walls, throw-away humor, claustrophobic action. Each touch, developed over years of practice, found a spot in The Sea Hawk.

Standing before a map of the world, King Philip of Spain (Montague Love) rages over England's blockage of his empire's expansion. He orders Don Alvarez (Claude Rains) to the queen's court, where Alvarez is to allay any fears the queen might have concerning the massing of Spain's war machine. In the meantime, the armada is preparing to invade England.

Don Alvarez and his niece, Dona Maria (Brenda Marshall), set sail for England, but Captain Geoffrey Thorpe's (Flynn) ship, the Albatross, intercepts their galleon. A furious sea battle ensues as the two vessels draw closer and blast each other. Beautifully edited and well-staged, the battle scene is a remarkable sequence. Thorpe and his men grapple with the Spanish galleon, then board her. In a tremendous flurry, the two crews clash with muskets, pistols, and swords. The scene is superior to a similar one in Captain Blood; Curtiz outdoes himself in terms of packed-in action. The fight rages until Thorpe tricks the Spaniards into surrender. Triumphant, the privateers capture Don Alvarez and Dona Maria prisoner, and free the English prisoners chained to the galleon's oars.

Everything to this point functions as the prologue of the film. The scene shifts to Queen Elizabeth's throne room, where the Queen (Flora Robson) denounces the actions of her Sea Hawks. To placate the furious Don Alvarez, she orders Captain Thorpe arrested and brought to her quarters. Together, they plan a daring raid on Spain's gold shipment from Panama. Spanish spy Lord Wolfingham (Henry Daniell, in what clearly should have been a role for Basil Rathbone) learns of their intrigue and plots with Don Alvarez to end the Sea Hawk's career once and for all. Dona Maria, now in love with Thorpe, tries to warn him. She commandeers a coach and speeds to the Albatross dock, but a town crier tells her she's too late. She stands on the pier, watching the morning mist envelop the departing ship. Thorpe stands at the rail, looking back towards England. As Korngold's love theme builds, Curtiz pulls his camera away from the

The Sea Hawk: Alan Hale (left) and Errol Flynn gloat over
the spoils of piracy.

anguished girl--drawing away from her just as Thorpe is (an
unusually tender moment for the director).

The Albatross arrives in Panama and the crew sets out
to seek their prize. Forewarned, the Spanish bait a trap
and snap it on the unsuspecting Englishmen. Many are
killed, but Thorpe and a few others fight their way through
the dense jungle back to the ship, only to be captured when
they board her. Quickly tried, they are sentenced, for
life, and ordered chained to the oars of a Spanish galleon.
Thus ends, it seems, the terror of the Sea Hawk.

Back in England, a gleeful Don Alvarez carries to the
queen the news of Thorpe's failure, only to have Dona
Maria collapse upon hearing the news. The Spanish ambassador is flustered and infuriated when the hard-edged queen
orders a portrait of King Philip removed from her sight.

Thorpe and the survivors of his crew escape their
chains and find that the ship they've been imprisoned on is

carrying secret instructions to Lord Wolfingham concerning
the impending invasion. They overwhelm the crew and sail
to warn England. A Spanish sympathizer warns Wolfingham
of Thorpe's return, and the palace guards are ordered to
stop the Sea Hawk from reaching the queen. It is
Wolfingham who blocks Thorpe, and the two foes square off
in a typical rapier duel. Across the darkened throne room,
upstairs, through glass doors, over tables, Curtiz follows
the action with his fluid camera movement. Furiously paced
and tightly edited, the sequence is Curtiz at his best,
presenting an eternally memorable image of Errol Flynn.
Thorpe runs Wolfingham through, and the enemy of England
falls dead at the base of the queen's throne. The queen,
disturbed by the sounds of battle and roused by Dona
Maria, saves Captain Thorpe from her personal guards.
Thorpe delivers the official dispatches intended for Wolfingham, thus insuring that England will not be caught unaware.
The film ends as the grateful queen knights her loyal servant and tells her cheering subjects that England will remain
free as long as there are men like him to protect her shores.

Needless to say, The Sea Hawk was a major hit. Storybook from end to end, the adventure never lets up; and the
film remains a classic of the genre. Despite his own reserva-
tions, Errol Flynn was unsurpassed in this type of role; he
cuts a dashing figure throughout, Curtiz having pushed all
the right buttons to bring out the star's potential. Claude
Rains lends strong support as the wily Don Alvarez. Dependable hands, Donald Crisp, Alan Hale, and the great Una
O'Connor, each shine in strong bits. Brenda Marshall, a
Warners contract player being pushed towards stardom, gives
a good account of herself as Thorpe's lover, Dona Maria.

Usually, women in Curtiz' films are either hard-
bitten or sarcastically bitchy. When exceptions pop up (Maid
Marian in Robin Hood, Dona Maria), they most often are
played too softly and sweetly to be believed. But Flora
Robson's Queen Elizabeth is a joy to watch. She struts
through most of her scenes with the solid authority of a true
monarch and is virtually "one of the boys." (Curtiz must
have encouraged her to beef up her character.)

Featuring a solid script, a top cast, a fine score, and
excellent production values, The Sea Hawk ranks as one of
the finest masterpieces in the Michael Curtiz gallery.

During production of The Sea Hawk, Curtiz was fortu-
nate in having access to a new water tank that had just been
constructed on Stage 21 of the Warner Bros. lot. The tank
was almost literally an interior manmade lake and capable of
holding water several feet deep. Many men (375) were employed in the construction of true-to-scale ships. The vessels were mounted on steel platforms connected to hydraulic
jacks, this in order to produce a rocking motion. The film
was not shot in Technicolor because the original plan (before
a budget increase) was to make use of stock footage from
the silent 1924 version of the feature. The Panamanian sequences were tinted sepia in selected first-release prints.
Flynn's double in some of the fencing shots was Don Turner.
Henry Daniell, because he was not adept at swordplay, in
most of his scenes used Ralph Faulker and Ned Davenport
as doubles. Brenda Marshall's singing voice was dubbed by
Sally Sweetland.

The budget for The Sea Hawk was approximately
$1,400,000. A shorter version of the film, cut by about
18 minutes, was reissued in 1947, although the complete version is the one which is currently distributed to television.

Santa Fe Trail (137)

Santa Fe Trail is the final Flynn/Curtiz western. It has
little more to offer than 110 minutes of time-killing entertainment.

Built around the antislavery campaigns of John Brown
(Raymond Massey), the scenario pits Union Army officer
Jeb Stuart (Flynn) and George Custer (Ronald Reagan)
against the abolitionist. As the saying goes, history was
never like this.

Perhaps unhappy with the disappointing Virginia City
(1940), Curtiz apparently put more effort into Santa Fe
Trail. There is true urgency in most of Massey's scenes,
and his fervor spills over the top. Massey's John Brown
completely engulfs Santa Fe Trail; His is one of the few
scenery-chewing performances in any Curtiz film.

Curtiz uses several scenes as build-ups to the Harper's
Ferry battle--the climatic centerpiece of the film. Near the

opening there is a nicely executed gun battle on a train, and an early John Brown raid is sharply told.

Everything else becomes padding. Both Stuart and Custer vie for the affections of "Kit" Carson Holliday (Olivia de Havilland). This competition leads to an obvious conclusion.

Flynn cronies Alan Hale and Guinn "Big Boy" Williams are on hand to lend so-called comic relief, but most of their material is almost painful to watch. One sequence stands out, however. Fellow army officers Stuart, Custer, Sheridan, Longstreet, Pickett, and Hood huddle around a Sioux Indian witch-woman's fire, as she speaks of a coming battle that will soon transform the six good friends into bitter enemies. Under-lit and provocatively scored, this is the single most effective scene in Santa Fe Trail.

The final battle at Harper's Ferry is well mounted and exciting. Waves of blue-coated soldiers advance into murderous fire, and Curtiz keeps the scene moving. As the situation becomes more desperate, John Brown becomes more unstable, until even his followers begin to fear him. He is finally captured by Stuart, and a quick trial brings a quicker verdict: John Brown must die to save the Union.

Errol Flynn pays more attention to his role in Santa Fe Trail than he paid to his part in Virginia City. He is more animated and even seems interested in projecting a full-blown character. Ronald Reagan does little more than hit the marks and say his lines, but this is, after all, Flynn's movie.

Though it was a hit for Flynn, Santa Fe Trail did little to the list of Michael Curtiz accomplishments.

The Sea Wolf (138)

Michael Curtiz sank his directorial teeth into the script of
The Sea Wolf. All the favorite Curtiz ingredients were laid
in--tension, conflict, action, and seemingly hopeless odds
to overcome--everything the director excelled at presenting.
Even an inevitable love interest thrown in by studio demand
couldn't break the tight emotional narrative. Most of the
action and reaction stemmed from the strengths (and one
fatal weakness) of the title character--Captain "Wolf"
Larsen.

From start to finish, the film moves at a fast, forceful
pace. Main characters are introduced, instantly defined,
and then quickly imprisoned aboard Larsen's sailing "hell-
ship," The Ghost. Thrown together to endure the last
voyage of the Sea Wolf are writer Humphrey Van Weyden
(Alexander Knox), escaped convict Ruth Brewster (Ida
Lupino), and fugitive George Leach (John Garfield). Garfield was a top star at the time, but he functioned in The
Sea Wolf mainly as a box-office draw, playing the love
interest for rising Warner star Ida Lupino. The actual
second male lead was Alexander Knox, whose intelligent,
sensitive performance provided a mirror to the often horri-
fying proceedings. Always observing, and privy to the
Captain's confidence, Van Weyden narrated the feature.

Sailing an erratic course, avoiding contact with other
ships, the crew begins to grow restless. Captain Larsen
incites incidents--partly to demonstrate his authority, partly
to satisfy his perverse nature.

While Van Weyden learns more about the enigmatic
ship's master, Ruth and Leach fall in love. They dream of
escape and freedom, but the shadow of Larsen hangs over
them.

Indeed, the shadow of Wolf Larsen hangs over the entire film. Edward G. Robinson gave perhaps his greatest
performance as the megalomaniacal captain. Ostensibly an
ugly, bestial brute, Larsen is cursed with what Van Weyden
calls "the ability to think." Intelligent, self-taught, constantly seeking justification for his actions, Robinson's
character rules his claustrophobic world with an iron hand.
Inspired by a passage from Milton's epic "Paradise Lost"

The Sea Wolf: Edward G. Robinson (center) aboard his
claustrophobic ship.

("Better to reign in hell than to serve in heaven"), he is a
complex mixture of wisdom and violence, of reason and anger.

Curtiz adroitly heightens every conflict. Grinning
coldly, reacting with obvious glee whenever he causes random violence to occur, the malevolent Larsen appears merci-
less. When Van Weyden strikes back at the insidious Cookie
(Barry Fitzgerald), the overjoyed captain urges the gentle
writer to "stick the knife in him." Later, when the captain
provokes the crew into tossing the same Cookie overboard
during a shark attack, Larsen surveys the wounds, and he
sneers, instructing the men to "patch up what's left of
his [Cookie's] leg." Hitting all the right notes in a difficult
role, Robinson's powerful, assured portrayal of the raging,
tormented captain elevates The Sea Wolf to classic heights.

After an attempt on Larsen's life fails, Ruth, Leach,
and Van Weyden, during one of the captain's spells of

blindness, manage to escape in a small boat. When the
Macedonia (captained by Larsen's brother, who has sworn to
kill the Sea Wolf) attacks, the crew learns at last of Larsen's
disability, and a mutiny ensues. The battered Ghost, empty
save for the now nearly-blind captain, drifts aimlessly.

Curtiz keeps the scenes flowing well throughout. Every
one, whatever its content, is sparked with nervous energy.
In the scene where the fugitives load their boat for escape,
the seemingly blind Captain stares blankly toward them. Later, when the now-crippled Cookie trips Larsen and cries,
"He's blind," the horrified Captain stands helpless and exposed. Curtiz pulls his camera in, closing up on Robinson's
face, which is contorted with fear.

The boat carrying the trio drifts back to the sinking
hulk of The Ghost. Leach goes aboard for provisions and is
trapped by the maniacal captain. Van Weyden confronts the
crazed Larsen and sacrifices himself for the lovers. The
Ghost sinks with the doomed Van Weyden and defiant Larsen
united in death.

The Sea Wolf, (with its pathological overtones) was
ahead of its time in 1941, but the public responded enthusiastically. Robinson's tour de force performance stands out
even today, and the supporting cast, too, rose to the occasion. Moody, fog-shrouded, and insightfully scored by
Erich Wolfgang Korngold, The Sea Wolf was a triumph for
Michael Curtiz.

Dive Bomber (139)

The year 1940 brought a new war to the United States.
President Roosevelt proclaimed isolationism and sent Britain
"lend-lease" destroyers. Hitler's armies swept across
France and stood ready to invade England. Americans
were violently divided between ties to their new country
and loyalties to homelands left behind. Hollywood studios,
many headed by Jewish businessmen, clearly saw the danger
posed by the Nazi war-machine and geared their studios
toward productions that would bring the message home to
every American. The result was a huge loss in the European market, but the word got on screen.

Dive Bomber was designed to show a powerful American
Navy constantly striving for technical improvement. Lieutenant Douglas Lee (Flynn) joins a team of flight surgeons
engaged in researching medical problems that have resulted
from high-altitude flying. Lee (Flynn), the dedicated
Dr. Rogers (Ralph Bellamy), and the skilled pilot Joe Blake
(Fred MacMurray) meet and conquer the "black-out in a
dive" problem that's been plaguing seasoned pilots. Blake
loses his life in the process, and Lee vows that Blake's sacrifice will not have been in vain.

Padding the overlong feature are scenes with Alexis
Smith, the pointless romantic interest who causes friction
between Lee and Blake. Allen Jenkins is cast as "Lucky"
James. Although he adds little to this feature, Jenkins is
one of those underrated character actors who made many
Warner Bros. movies a joy to watch. With his sardonic face
and perpetual grimace, he was a quintessential Curtiz stock
figure.

Dive Bomber was the final Flynn/Curtiz film. The
men refused to work with each other on any more productions. Their collaboration had helped elevate Flynn to the
stature of a top star, yet most of Flynn's best films were
behind him. Curtiz moved on to more studio assignments,
and, if he missed Errol Flynn at all, no one ever noticed it.

Captains of the Clouds (140)

Like Dive Bomber (1941), Captains of the Clouds was a call-
to-action epic designed to fan patriotic flames. Produced
before America entered the war, the film spotlighted the efforts of the Royal Canadian Air Force to aid England. From
star (Cagney) to score (Max Steiner) to Technicolor
photography (Polito & Cline), the studio went all out to give
the feature full "A" treatment.

James Cagney was at the height of his box-office
popularity when Captains of the Clouds was listed on the
shooting schedule; the film was a full-blown star vehicle for
him. Curtiz pits Cagney's character Brian MacLean against
everyone and everything. A crack bush pilot, MacLean joins
the service and learns military discipline the hard way.
Supremely confident in his flying abilities, his enforced

education in "how to function on a team" forms the basis of
the film. Each incident serves to teach the brash pilot the
importance of following orders and performing assigned
duties. Swaggering, almost obnoxious, MacLean grows to
understand the military code and by the end of the story,
becomes a true "team player." The part is pure Cagney,
and Curtiz points him in the right direction throughout.

Praised by the public and critics for its soaring
aerial sequences as well as for Cagney's performance, the
message of Captains of the Clouds comes across with typical
Curtiz bluntness: sometimes the individual must be sacri-
ficed for the greater good of his country. Because of
movies like this one, Americans who would soon be asked to
make their sacrifice understood more clearly the reasons
behind their choice of action.

The overall upbeat feel of the script prevented Curtiz
from projecting much of his usual hard-bitten cynicism into
the scenes. As a result, the film, peopled by stock characters acting out stereotypical roles, is a tightly-knit testimony
to patriotic fervor; though it may be a triumph of technique,
the movie is definitely not a stand-out Curtiz effort.

Yankee Doodle Dandy (141)

When James Cagney's name is mentioned, most people usually
remember his power, his dynamic screen presence. Trained
in acting and dancing for the Broadway stage, he was given
the title role in The Public Enemy (1931) only as an after-
thought. But because depression-era audiences responded
to the flamboyant Irishman, he quickly became a top-rank
star. On screen, he was the guy from the wrong side of the
tracks--from the slums, from the reform schools--who was just
one step away from the Big House and two away from the gas
chamber. He was a regular guy who made it good and carved
out a name for himself, and millions of jobless people lived on
the hope that perhaps they, too, could catch some of the same
lightning in a bottle.

Cagney was sure of himself. Throughout most of his
long tenure at Warner Bros. he was a constant thorn in Jack
Warner's side. The actor knew his value as a box-office draw
and used it as a crowbar to open the studio safe. But even

Yankee Doodle Dandy: James Cagney.

the hard-bitten Warner acknowledged that the versatile
Cagney always gave 110 percent in everything he appeared
in.

Yankee Doodle Dandy was a project that demanded 110
percent effort.   George M. Cohan was already an American
show business legend in 1942, even more so than the
revered Al Jolson.

Today, Cohan is regarded as more of a myth than a
man.   In fact, it's difficult for most people to even imagine
the entertainment world Cohan starred in so brightly.
There was no television medium to over-expose his act and
few records to spread and diffuse his talent.   To reach the
heights of the vaudeville Valhalla, people had to see you
perform and remember your impact.

Few achieved high rank, but Cohan towered over them all. It was only natural that, sooner or later, Hollywood would seek to present his screen biography. But the head-strong trouper held out for years. He insisted on a premium price for screen rights and demanded cast approval--especially as to who would portray the Yankee Doodle Boy himself. Swiftly declining health spurred the ailing star to finally consummate a film deal, and Warner Bros. won out because the studio had the one man Cohan believed could do him justice--James Cagney.

Certainly Cagney could dance. He'd proven that in more than a few films. But now he had to imitate an icon's style--a style that hundreds of thousands of nostalgic people fondly remembered. In later years, Cagney would stress that he'd decided from the outset to imitate Cohan in stage production numbers, but not in off-stage scenes. The combination of George M. Cohan's bombastic stage style and Jimmy Cagney's acting bravura set the pace for Yankee Doodle Dandy.

Michael Curtiz was virtually the only studio director who could handle the assignment. For all his cynicism, the Hungarian expatriate's work reflected a surprisingly passionate love for his adopted country. And that's what Yankee Doodle Dandy is, a love story--the love of a man (and all men) for America, and, in turn, the love America returns to a man who gives everything for his country.

Put into production just as the United States entered World War II, Yankee Doodle Dandy attempts to show what an entire generation of drafted soldiers would soon be asked to fight (and die) for. Earlier Curtiz films tried to do that (Dive Bomber, Captains of the Clouds), but none shouted the message more proudly than Yankee Doodle Dandy. Purely American, completely nationalistic, fully entertaining, the film was a box-office smash and reportedly held a permanent place on FDR's White House film list.

The United States is mobilizing for the Second World War when show business great George M. Cohan is called to the White House from the dressing room of his latest Broadway hit. Shaken, the humble Irish-American makes his way to Washington and is ushered into an audience with President Roosevelt. In flashback, the actor tells the story of the four Cohans.

Curtiz handles the prologue smoothly. His camera follows two critics into the theater as the two men discuss the latest Cohan flag-waving show. Each major character gets a strong introduction, as the director establishes their roles. Cagney plays the aged entertainer with graceful restraint and casts an engaging image from the start. Joan Leslie, portraying Cohan's ever-faithful wife, Mary, shines as a beacon of understanding. (In fact, however, the character was an amalgam, since Cohan was actually married more than once in real life.) Richard Whorf, a Warners contract player, later to become a successful producer/director, acquits himself well in support of Cagney. His solid portrayal of faithful friend and business partner Sam Harris is an unexpected plus to the feature. In fact, many featured cast actors contribute unusually strong performances. Curtiz coaxed top bits from Rosemary DeCamp (George's mother, Nellie), Irene Manning (Broadway star Fay Templeton), and Jimmy Cagney's sister, screen newcomer Jeanne Cagney (George M. Cohan's sister). Fleshing out the film and contributing strong showings were other familiar Warner Bros. stock company players: George Tobias, S. Z. Sakall, Walter Catlett, and Frank Faylen. Each fit into the romanticized texture of the film.

Old-time troupers Jerry Cohan (Walter Huston) and his wife Nellie build a family while touring the vaudeville circuit. They work their children into their soft-shoe routines and see that eldest son George displays a natural ability for show business.

As the children grow, so does the expanding country. The "Four Cohans" act becomes a box-office draw, in time sophisticated enough to aspire to Broadway.

As a salute to Cohan, the scriptwriters worked overtime, sentimentalizing the developing years of Cohan's career. The mainspring of the team's drive is Cohan's father, a true vaudevillian dedicated to the theater. Curtiz details the Irish patriarch as a saintly patriot who guides his close-knit family through rough times.

Walter Huston clearly had a grand time with the part. The veteran actor worked hard to project his character's necessary strength and drive, as well as to show the elder Cohan as a talented entertainer. Dancing, doing soft-shoe

Yankee Doodle Dandy: Joan Leslie and James Cagney.

patter, following the director through a series of year-
condensing sequences--Huston earned a well-deserved Best
Supporting Actor nomination for his performance.

   The family's act is stymied due to George's headstrong
temperament; producers refuse to book the team as long as
he is included.   The Cohans drift into reclusion, but the
still-proud family refuses to exclude the young Cohan.
Through sheer gall and a timely teaming with young Sam
Harris, George manages to secure financing for his first
big show--Yankee Doodle Dandy.   The show is a smash hit,
the audiences eagerly accepting what critics deride as vulgar
flag-waving.   One success leads to another, and finally the
Four Cohans part company.   Supported by his wife, Mary,
George M. Cohan becomes a solo act.

   Cagney and Curtiz go all out for the musical sequences.
The staging of "You're a Grand Old Flag" approaches mythic
proportions.   What seem like thousands of extras hoist

American flags and march across a stage that could only exist in a Hollywood studio. Cagney's dynamic dancing punctuates the spectacle, and a huge flag is projected on the
curtain when it falls. The image is fixed and lasting, a
tribute to the Curtiz vision. Other songs are nicely staged;
the film presents each in smooth succession. Among the
featured songs are "Mary's a Grand Old Name," "Harrigan,"
"Forty-five Minutes from Broadway," and "Give My Regards
to Broadway." There's a brilliant moment during the
"Yankee Doodle Boy" sequence--the exuberant Cohan dances
from stage right towards stage left, and his momentum carries him up the stage wall. Curtiz drops his camera down
to heighten the angle on the movement, and the throwaway
action creates an exciting effect.

The flag-waving and patriotic fervor heightened the
feelings of the time. World War II had just begun, and the
stirring rendition of "Over There" performed the same service in the '40s that it had in 1917. There was a job to do,
and millions of American soldiers stood ready to do it. Set
in an Army camp, the number was given added flourishes by
Curtiz. Cagney, with singer Frances Langford, leads
massed troops during the song. When the generator fails,
hundreds of truck lights are used to light the scene. The
stage becomes a veritable outdoor concert hall, and, when
the song ends, the joyous soldiers toss their hats into the
air, cheering.

After a fabulous and noteworthy career, Cohan drifts
into retirement, almost forgotten by the public. Mary
schemes to coax him out so he can help financially troubled
Sam Harris. The show Cohan agrees to do is I'd Rather Be
Right, a lampoon of President Roosevelt's long tenure in
office. The aged Cohan is a hit again, and then the letter
from the White House arrives.

The flashback sequence ends, and the actor apologizes
to the president for taking up so much of his time. In a
ringing speech, F.D.R. commends the entire Cohan saga and
bestows upon the stunned entertainer the Presidential Medal--
the highest decoration presented to civilians. At an unac-
customed loss for words, the actor recovers enough to accept
the award and says his family's trademark closing line, "My
mother thanks you, my father thanks you, my sister thanks
you, and I thank you." He assures the President that he's

just begun to earn the medal, and with that he takes his
leave. But there is one flourish left. On the way down the
White House stairs, the exuberant Cohan kicks into a little
jig that puts a capper on the night's events. Strutting
proudly out into the street, he then joins a parade of troops
singing "Over There."

Of all the special moments in Yankee Doodle Dandy, the
brief dance down the White House stairs ranks as one of the
finest. A vivid expression of joy and pride in a job well-
done, the dance sums up the entire film.

Naturally, Yankee Doodle Dandy was a big hit for everyone involved. It became Jimmy Cagney's all-time highest
grossing movie and earned him his only Academy Award.
Michael Curtiz, earning another nomination for his inspired
direction, fell short again and did not bring home an Oscar.
Yankee Doodle Dandy, nevertheless, continues to shine today.
The film stands as a tribute to an American institution and
to the American spirit.

●   ●   ●

Mission to Moscow (142) is a propagandistic look at the real-
life events surrounding Ambassador Joseph Davies' stay in
Russia. The screenplay was adapted from Davies' memoirs,
and Davies himself introduces the film in a prologue. Although
the movie became notorious in the McCarthy era as a result of
its pro-Soviet stance, at the time of its release, Mission to
Moscow accurately reflected America's friendly view toward
Russia and managed to present that view with stylistic flourish.

This is the Army (143) is a splashy Technicolor military
musical. It's packed with skits and bouncy songs, and is very
enjoyable on its own terms. This movie was followed by the
film that is undeniably Curtiz' most famous and (arguably) his
most accomplished.

Casablanca (144)

It was Casablanca that, finally, earned Curtiz an Oscar as
Best Director. What started out as a "B" feature starring

Ronald Reagan and Ann Sheridan turned out to be Curtiz'
magnum opus.

Humphrey Bogart had only recently escaped the contract
treadmill. A Warners stock player since 1936, he'd made high
marks with the studio hierarchy by accepting just about every
script offered to him. Some of them were painfully ludicrous.
He played a wrestling promoter in Swing Your Lady (1938),
a sneering, black-clad Western bad-guy in The Oklahoma Kid
(1939), and an Irish groom in Dark Victory (1940), but,
nevertheless, he came up through the ranks and gained
needed experience before the cameras.

Several fine Warners directors helped to mold Bogart's
screen persona. Raoul Walsh recommended Bogart for High
Sierra (1941), a hit that brought fresh public interest to the
fading gangster cycle. John Huston wrote and directed what
is now considered the classic remake of Dashiell Hammett's
The Maltese Falcon (1941); in that film, Huston made Bogart
a bankable romantic lead. It was left to Michael Curtiz to
round off the remaining rough edges and add the final
touches to Bogart's screen image. Bogart's Casablanca
character, Rick Blaine, became the quintessential Bogie
incarnation--a tough, world-weary, cynical man, self-governed
by a private code of honor and susceptible to a vulnerable
romanticism. Every Bogart role from Casablanca on would be
a variation of the main theme established in Rick's Café
Americain.

The plot of Casablanca is well known enough to be considered folklore. Suffice it to say that the story is a heady
mixture of politics, soap opera, and espionage laced with
self-sacrifice. Curtiz keeps the film's narrative drive moving
forward at breakneck speed (later he would say that he had
to, in order to conceal the holes in the plot). This frantic
pace is maintained, and maintained well, for the picture's
entire 102 minutes, as all the tangled story threads are wo-
ven neatly into place and resolved by one of the most satisfying climaxes in movie history. Textured and complex, the
finished product is a remarkable achievement by any standard
and a supreme example of the Hollywood studio machine oper-
ating at peak efficiency.

Curtiz chose to emphasize the romantic torment of the
Bogart character, relegating the Second World War to mere

Casablanca: Paul Henreid (left), Ingrid Bergman, and
Humphrey Bogart.

background status. Haunted by a song ("As Time Goes By")
and happy memories of Ilsa in Paris, the now disillusioned
and politically neutral Rick proclaims, "I stick my neck out
for no one." A rich Max Steiner score is equally effective
to Arthur Edeson's sumptuous photography as Curtiz flashes
back to the source of Rick's disillusionment.

Jilted by the woman he loves, the heartbroken expatriate is left standing in the rain, as his loyal friend Sam
(Dooley Wilson) pulls him aboard the last train to leave
Paris before the invading Nazi Army marches into the city.
Later in the film, when Ilsa confronts Rick with a gun and
demands the vital letters of transit, he opens his coat and
says, "Go ahead and shoot. You'll be doing me a favor."
On the edge of being maudlin, this material was redeemed
by the cast's inspired response to Curtiz' direction.

Ingrid Bergman was borrowed from the Selznick contract stable, and she contributed a fine performance as the
loyal Ilsa. Torn between Rick and the admirable Laszlo
(Paul Henreid), she played out her part with grace and un-
decidedness, heightening the tension leading to the airport
finale. Claude Rains plays Captain Louis Renault, Casablanca's prefect of police and Rick's friend. Perhaps the
only Frenchman with a cultured English accent, Renault
functions as Rick's conscience. Always on hand with a wry
comment or a small wager ("I'm only a poor corrupt official"),
Rains turns in an admirable, near-flawless performance, ad-
ding subterranean menace to Renault's surface friendliness.

The remainder of the cast forms a wonderful ensemble,
each actor managing to bring life to characters that would
have been far less impressive under the guidance of most
other directors. Paul Henreid, an often stolid actor, gives
Victor Laszlo depth and molds the character to almost heroic
proportions. Conrad Veidt, near the end of a long and dis-
tinguished career, is perfect as the cold Nazi Major Strasser.
Dooley Wilson, a relative unknown, provides solid support as
Rick's piano-playing friend--and this at a time when many
black actors were still restricted to playing cabbies and por-
ters. Other Warner Bros. contract players fleshed out the
film: Sydney Greenstreet, Peter Lorre, S. Z. Sakall, Leonid
Kinsky, Ludwig Stossel, Marcel Dalio, Helmut Dantine, John
Qualen, Madeline LeBeau, all of them investing their parts
with flashes of brilliance.

Casablanca is a director's film, and a weaker director
could not have produced the same results that Curtiz produced. Even today, after Rick has shot Major Strasser so
that Ilsa and Victor can escape, audiences cheer when Renault
instructs his men to "Round up the usual suspects." The
break in tension is cathartic at that point, and when the two

Casablanca: Humphrey Bogart (left) and Peter Lorre.

Casablanca: Dooley Wilson (left), Humphrey Bogart, and
Ingrid Bergman.

friends, united in purpose, walk off together into the airport
fog, it's not just an ending, it's Michael Curtiz writing "finis"
to his finest epic.

Passage to Marseilles (145)

Considering the top cast and the obvious French connection
suggested by its title, viewers might have assumed that this
film would be the long-awaited sequel to Casablanca. Not so.
Passage to Marseilles owes nothing to any film before it, yet
is in itself a remarkable movie. Richly textured, lightly
executed, and functional on several levels, it offered both
Humphrey Bogart and Michael Curtiz interesting challenges.

Though Bogart was a major star, this film places him
in an ensemble piece, where he becomes a part, not the whole,
of the story. Several distinct tales are told, and Matrac's
(Bogart) forms the base that all the others grow from.

In this movie, Bogart must go it alone. Unlike his role
in Casablanca, there is no leading lady, no Ingrid Bergman
to play against or to anchor to. Michele Morgan plays Matrac's
wife, Paula, but she throws in only a thread, not a lifeline.
To be exact, La Belle France is the leading lady of this film.
It is she who rallies her lost men, using honor and national
pride as her call.

Curtiz attacked the script, cutting the diverse elements
into sharp sequences. Employing an unusual flashback technique (even by today's standards), he explains each
principal's motivation in simple terms.

Hearing of France's entry into war with Germany,
Matrac and four other Devil's Island convicts--Marius (Peter
Lorre), Renault (Philip Dorn), Petit (Helmut Dantine) and
Garon (George Tobias)--escape in hopes of joining the fight
for their home country. Their canoe is picked up by a
French freighter on which they meet Capt. Freycinet (Claude
Rains) and run afoul of Nazi sympathizer Major Duval (Sydney
Greenstreet). This footage functions as a flashback, and
Curtiz employs flashbacks within the flashback to tell each
convict's story.

Each man is guilty of one sort of crime or another.

We learn that Matrac was an idealistic newspaper publisher
who loved his country but not her government. He was
framed for murder and locked away, bitter and disillusioned.
The coming of war has convinced Matrac that France still
has hope; he wants to help fan the flames of nationalism,
but his faith is shattered when word comes over the radio
that his country has surrendered and all ships must be
turned over to the Vichy authorities.

The passengers and crew become violently divided.
Some want to comply with the order. Others wish to sail
for England and join the free French army being formed
there. Duval settles the argument by leading a mutiny of
the Nazi sympathizers, who try to take control of the ship.
Matrac and his fellow convicts help put down the uprising,
but not before Duval is able to radio the German air force
for help. Bombers attack the fleeing vessel, and Marius is
killed. The rest finally reach England, where all of them
join the free French air force.

The imapct of this nationalistic battlecry is felt even
now. Curtiz saw the power between the lines of the story
and was more than able to bring it to the surface. Each
convict lusts to defend the very country that has cast him
out. Each man risks his life to expel invaders from the
cities that have rejected him. Each character desperately
wants to return to the land where he was born. By placing
the convicts in the air force, Curtiz denies them the opportunity to touch home soil until the war ends. Of all ironies,
this is one that Curtiz emphasizes most cruelly.

The final irony has yet to be shown. While the free
French squadron returns from a raid over occupied territory,
Freycinet learns that Renault's plane has been delayed.
After the mission, the plane altered course so that Matrac
could drop a packet to his wife. The message is never de-
livered. Badly shot up, the plane limps back to home base,
barely able to land. Matrac has died in transit, and over
the patriot's grave, Freycinet reads the letter Matrac intended for the son he has never seen. The fight will go on.

With powerful grace, Bogart plays the tormented Matrac.
A peaceful man driven by injustice and outrage to fight for
his country, he virtually explodes during scenes. At one
point, he machine-guns Nazi airmen off the wings of their

downed plane. His eyes flash hatred as they fall, and it is
clear that these Germans are just the first of many who will
die at his hands. Peter Lorre is fine as the cynical Marius--
the least convincing patriot of the lot. His heroic death spot-
lights the fact that sometimes men must die for their country.
Claude Rains is the old warrior Freycinet, who has been
through all this before and fancies he will see it all again.
Sydney Greenstreet is deliciously evil as the strutting Duval,
a man as stupid as he is shallow.

With the ease of a master, Curtiz mixes his pace. The
story never suffers and keeps moving towards its inevitable
end. Passage to Marseilles is a triumph of technique, due
mostly to the director's feel for the material. This is Michael
Curtiz at his best, elevating a good story into a great film.

•   •   •

Janie (146) is a pleasant comedy about a small-town girl
(Joyce Reynolds) who falls in love with a soldier. The film
was followed by Mildred Pierce (147), a movie adapted from
James M. Cain's novel. Joan Crawford won an Oscar for her
performance as Mildred, and although the film's attempted
middle-class atmosphere is at times undermined by inappro-
priately expensive sets and costumes, Curtiz' attention to
detail and his careful control over his actors' performances
raise the film above the ordinary. Mildred Pierce is a soap
opera, but classifying it as one seems almost insulting because the movie is certainly one of the finest soap operas
ever made.

Released in late 1945, Mildred Pierce was Curtiz' last
"big" popular success. From this point on, he would
settle into a comfortable period of decline, working on
equally prestigious and still-successful movies, but achieving
far less with them.

After Mildred Pierce, Curtiz directed Roughly Speaking
(148), a fairly amusing, but drawn-out comedy, starring
Rosalind Russell and Jack Carson.

The Gradual Decline

Night and Day (149)

One of the hardest problems to overcome in producing a
musical biopic is knowing just how to work the music in.
For Night and Day, the writers found a simple solution:
feature the songs and intersperse spots of drama. The
"solution" didn't work. Neither did the presence of Cole
Porter songs and Cary Grant as leading man. Night and
Day was Curtiz' only release of 1946; even so he was
limited to directing only the dramatic passages. The musical sequences were shot by LeRoy Prinz.

The film traces Porter's rise to Broadway eminence
from his early years at Yale, and it runs a predictable
course. The composer's early setback (World War I closes
his first show) and an unhappy courtship (he's not good
enough for her) are handled heavily. Cary Grant is too
leaden to make the character seem real. Too often he re-
lies on a flashy smile or on a nervous laugh to convey his
feelings. He had never worked under Curtiz, and Night
and Day's weak script gave him little room to build on.
Alexis Smith (Linda) co-stars as the woman who loves and
marries Porter, only to leave him because of his obsession
with perfection. Smith's limited acting range actually
helps her in this film. She projects a single-minded devo-
tion to the man, and not to his fame. Porter reaches the
height of his profession only to lose his wife. His work
provides little solace, and it takes a tragic crippling acci-
dent to reunite the couple. The film ends as the two
embrace in a garden, the Yale Glee Club singing the title
song.

Curtiz tried to squeeze punch out of the script, but
his efforts fell far short. There's just no flesh to cover

the bones of the plot.   Night and Day remains a beautiful
film to listen to.

Life with Father (150)

Based on a long-running stage play, Life With Father is one
of the most fondly remembered postwar movies of the Curtiz
filmography.   Owing to the success of the play, Warner Bros.
once again went all out in retaining the full flavor of the
original material.   Curtiz took a naturally good script and
fleshed out the characters.

William Powell, head of the Day household, up to that
point in his career was generally regarded as a veteran
lead.   On screen virtually throughout the film, Powell played
the irascible patriarch with gleeful elan.   His presence sparks
the film, and even when he is off-screen, the characters act
as though he's about to burst in on them.   Powell, an accomplished light comedian, worked hard with Curtiz to bring
the overbearing but lovable central character to the screen.
They tried to keep Powell's performance from spilling over
the top and sweeping the rest of the cast under, and they
were successful.   Irene Dunne was part of that success.
Her gentle underplaying of the almost saintly Mrs. Day adds
the balance needed to keep Powell in line.   She functions as
a completely good, strong, and fully capable woman (unusual
characterization for Curtiz).   The film follows the efforts of
the redhaired family to have their father baptized; it also
traces the coming of age of one of the young sons.   The
story is set around the turn of the century, and, with natural charm, moves gracefully through sequence after sequence.
The director injected few of his usual trademarks, preferring
to play up the gentle humor of the script.   The result is a
completely entertaining production, which exudes a warmth
uncommon for Curtiz.   With an assured built-in audience,
naturally the film was well received; it added to the reputation of all involved.

•   •   •

The Unsuspected (151) stars Claude Rains as a radio star
who tries to murder his niece (Joan Caulfield).   The role
Rains plays in this film provided a welcome change of pace
for him.   Usually he found himself in a supporting part.

The Unsuspected: Claude Rains (left) and Jack Lambert.

In The Unsuspected (as in other films) he is excellent, although the film itself doesn't quite measure up to his performance.

     The Unsuspected was followed by two musicals of about
equal quality, Romance on the High Seas (152) and My Dream
Is Yours (153). Both feature Warner Bros. musical starlet
Doris Day. The two movies are pleasant, though not memorable; and it is worth noting that Miss Day (whose whole-
some image would grow so tiresome in later years that she
would become an unintentional self-parody) comes off quite
well in these two films because she is allowed to play believable roles in an honest manner.

     After Flamingo Road (154) (another well-mounted Joan
Crawford soaper, this time with Sidney Greenstreet in support), Curtiz stepped in front of the camera for a change
and contributed an amusing cameo (playing himself) to the
comedy It's a Great Feeling (1949)--a mild Hollywood satire
starring Dennis Morgan, Doris Day, and Jack Carson.

Flamingo Road: Joan Crawford confronts Sydney Greenstreet as David Brian (center) looks on.

The Breaking Point: John Garfield (right).

Curtiz' next group of films remained competent, but mostly unimpressive. The Lady Takes a Sailor (155) is a comedy starring Jane Wyman; Young Man with a Horn (156) is a drama starring Kirk Douglas and Lauren Bacall that is inspired by the life of trumpeter Bix Beiderbecke; Bright Leaf (157) is a drama involving a tobacco farmer (Gary Cooper; and, The Breaking Point (158), starring John Garfield and Patricia Neal, is a superlative refilming of Ernest Hemingway's To Have and Have Not, which had been a Humphrey Bogart vehicle six years earlier.

The earlier picture had benefited from Bogart's presence and Howard Hawks' direction as well as from William Faulkner's and Jules Furthman's dialogue, but The Breaking Point is the superior of the two versions, with John Garfield and Juano Hernandez turning in dynamic performances and creating one of those rare instances when a movie remake surpasses an original film version.

Jim Thorpe-All American (159)

Hailed as the "greatest athlete of the century," Jim Thorpe was a natural subject for a Hollywood biopic. Burt Lancaster was in the middle of a production deal at Warners and seemed a perfect choice for the lead role in Thorpe's life story. The script Curtiz accepted, however, presented an interesting challenge.

As a young man, Thorpe had swept the 1912 Olympics. The screenwriters showed him reaching the heights early. Then they chronicled his descent into disgrace and obscurity. Olympic training was focused on as the young reservation-born Indian's obsession. Yet the actual Olympics are presented almost in passing.

Triumphant, Thorpe receives accolades from the King of Sweden. Then he returns home to cheering throngs. His triumph is short-lived, though; someone learns that Thorpe took money to play summer baseball. He is no longer an "amateur" by Olympic rules and, defamed in the public eye, is quickly stripped of his gold medals. A rapid bitter decline follows, as the proud Thorpe battles to retain his dignity and regain his trophies.

●   ●   ●

Jim Thorpe--All American: Burt Lancaster (center).

After Force of Arms (160), an updated remake of Farewell
to Arms starring William Holden and Nancy Olson, Curtiz
directed The Story of Will Rogers (161), starring Will
Rogers, Jr. as his father (this film is one of the few successful show business biographies).   It was followed by
I'll See You in My Dreams (162), another Doris Day musical,
and biography of songwriter Gus Kahn (played by the irri-
tating Danny Thomas).   Thomas was also featured in the
title role of The Jazz Singer (163), Curtiz' next effort.   A
sufficient but superfluous remake of the legendary Jolson
picture, the story was maudlin when Jolson did it in 1927,
and by 1953 the material hadn't improved with age.   The
Jolson charisma, enhanced by the novelty of sound, had been
at the core of the original's success, so when the same shaky
dramatic framework was rebuilt around the mawkish Danny
Thomas, it collapsed.   The Jazz Singer was followed, in mid-
1953, by a John Wayne picture that would be Curtiz' last effort under his Warner Bros. contract (although he would
return to the studio once more on a freelance basis to film
The Helen Morgan Story).

Trouble Along the Way (164)

Trouble Along the Way has the distinction of being one of
the weakest features John Wayne ever starred in during his
stint at Warner Bros.--a period that had produced popular
successes (Hondo, Island in the Sky) as well as critically
acclaimed films (The Searchers, High and the Mighty).
Essentially a "B" movie, the mere presence of Wayne elevated
the film's status (this marks the only time Curtiz would
direct John Wayne while working at Warners though the rest
of the cast is prime studio stock.

The story revolves around a favorite Hollywood cliché:
St. Anthony's College is being closed down within six months
unless it can clear up its debts. Father Burke (Charles
Coburn) decides that football is the only way to raise funds
in a hurry. Realizing that his athletic progrma is in total
collapse, Father Burke seeks the services of ex-pro coach
Steve Williams (Wayne). Reluctant at first, Williams finally
accepts the post when his ex-wife threatens to seize custody
of their daughter on the grounds that Williams is an unfit
guardian. He brings a hard-nosed approach to the sleepy
college ("Winning isn't everything, it's the only thing!") and
whips the football team into shape. Curtiz emphasizes the
rebuilding and rebirth angles, and the Wayne character
grows along with the team's strength. Social worker Alice
Singleton (Donna Reed) adds tension to the plot; she shows
up in the role of Williams' ex-wife's agent and soon falls for
the coach, aiding him in the fight to keep his daughter.

Pressures build. They reach their peak during the
climatic football match with Santa Clara. St. Anthony wins
the game and the school earns enough to pay its bills.
Wayne's methods are vindicated, but, as happens so often
in Curtiz films, victory quickly turns sour. Steve resigns
after arguing with Father Burke; his ex-wife sues for
custody. Bitter and beaten, Williams offers no defense, and
the court rules to take his child away. Friends come through
for Williams, though--both Alice and Father Burke rally to
his cause and romance wins out. Steve promises to return
to his coaching duties the next season but says he will be
taking a prolonged honeymoon. A new job and a new wife
on the horizon assures the return of Williams' daughter.

Trouble Along the Way, besides being so hackneyed,

bumps along at a disjointed pace. Saddled with a young
daughter, Wayne seems uneasy throughout most of the film.
His stiffness is no match for Reed's sweetness or Coburn's
piety. With little action to direct, Curtiz loses the feel of
the film, and the result is a strangely sentimental atmosphere. Trouble Along the Way is an aptly named movie.

•   •   •

After Trouble Along the Way came The Boy from Oklahoma
(165), Curtiz' first picture away from Warner Bros. The
subdued western stars Will Rogers, Jr. as a pacifist sheriff.

The Egyptian (166)

Edmund Purdom was one of the last victims of the Hollywood
big-star build-up machine. Big-time agents and T.V.
spelled doom for the studio assembly lines. Studio-nurtured
talent was becoming past history. Purdom, a capable actor
with moderate screen presence, could well have achieved
higher rank if he hadn't been thrust into disasters like The
Egyptian.

Hollywood producers were nearly in a panic during the
'50s. Eagerly, they cast around for fading box-office magic.
Musicals sold, so everyone made musicals. Westerns made a
comeback, so everyone made westerns. Three-D and
Cinemascope sold tickets, so everyone bought new camera
lenses. The Egyptian was born out of the public's acceptance
of wide-screen epics.

Michael Curtiz returned to the genre for the first time
since Noah's Ark (1929). The wide sweep of The Egyptian
story afforded many opportunities for both cast and director,
but the production nearly collapses under the heavy-handed
script.

The film traces the rise of Purdom to Pharoah, and it
details the increasingly complex interactions with his power-
hungry friend (Mature) and loyal physician (Wilding). Curtiz
created his wide-screen compositions with care. He edged
good performances out of Gene Tierney and Peter Ustinov.
But the overlong and preachy movie fails to sustain much

direction or drive, leaving little more to remember than good
sets and pleasant scenery.

Purdom plays the wise, but doomed, Pharoah with a
waxen face and monotone voice. His ineffectiveness is almost
matched by Victor Mature's sorry performance as the power-
mad friend. Mature coasts through the film with his usual
repertoire of one-note tricks. (Limited in ability but always
bankable, the dependable star enjoyed new popularity
throughout the '50s.)

At this time in his freelance career, Michael Curtiz was
in the same position the studios were in--he was looking for
fresh box-office magic.

White Christmas (167)

White Christmas, another '50s musical, packed with stock
characters and overflowing with sentiment, is a success in
spite of itself. Curtiz took a script that partially reworked
the classic Holiday Inn (1942), added fluffy Irving Berlin
tunes and a competent cast, (Bing Crosby, Danny Kaye,
Vera-Ellen, Rosemary Clooney), then molded the potentially
maudlin story into a lighthearted, well-rounded movie.

Army veterans Crosby and Kaye try to help their ex-
commanding officer (Dean Jagger) make a success of his
rundown winter resort. Along the way they encounter the
usual problems, but in the end goodwill and friendship win
out, and each man finds romance.

Curtiz paced his directorial credit for White Christmas
over a shot of a showgirls' propped-up, black-stockinged
legs. This slightly racy ploy contrasted sharply with the
film's gentle feel and pointed out the director's apparent dis-
satisfaction with frothy assignments.

We're No Angels (168)

Given the full "A" treatment and peopled with an imposing
cast of talent, We're No Angels should have been more entertaining. As it stands, however, the film is a well-mixed bag
of weary cynicism and Yuletide cheer.

Three Devil's Island convicts, Joseph (Bogart), Albert (Ray), and Jules (Ustinov) escape prison and hide out in a store managed by Felix Ducotel (Leo G. Carroll). Disguised as laborers, the convicts scheme to kill the shopkeeper and his family and then to escape the island on the next boat. The plan proves impossible; the family members are so sweet and friendly that the convicts decide to help them instead.

Curtiz moves the action from point A to point B, content with playing up the comic aspects of the Ustinov character. The film lacks any spark until the greedy uncle, Andre Trochard (Rathbone), arrives on Christmas Eve, intent on going over the hopelessly tangled books and installing his insipid nephew Paul in Felix' place. A drastic change of pace kicks in, and the feel of the piece turns to one of urgent disarray. In quick succession, Rathbone and his nephew are neatly disposed of by Albert's pet snake, Adolf. ("Adolf, we salute you.") The convicts find a lover for Felix' daughter, and the entire family business reverts to Felix as a result of Uncle Andre's death.

Curtiz treats the three convicts as benevolent forces of good (singly, and as a group). Their actions are dictated by the circumstances they walk into, and their responses are alternately funny and hard-edged.

The convicts steal a Christmas tree and the governor's prize turkey. Bogart collects a delinquent debt from a regular customer and tries to sell a hairbrush set to a bald man. Ustinov pursues a frumpy woman so diligently that she flees the shop. Aldo Ray awakens Isabelle's sexual feelings but decides she is much too good for him. The three men become a mixture of the Three Wise Men and Santa Claus, benefiting the deserving family at the cost (almost) of their new-found freedom.

The film ends as the three convicts are about to escape the Island. After quick reflection, they decide to head back to jail. ("You meet a better class of people there.") As they begin the long walk back to the prison, halos appear, in turn, above each of their heads--there's even a tiny one for Adolf.

Based on a play, We're No Angels is clearly a set-piece conceived as frothy holiday fare. Humphrey Bogart might not have been the right choice for the lead, but, reunited with

Curtiz for the first time since Passage to Marseilles (1944), the star turned in a workmanlike performance. Aldo Ray is strangely subdued as Albert, but Peter Ustinov is a joy to watch. His character, Jules, lusts after a "fine fat lady" and expresses shame about his amazing ability to open any locked safe or door. Curtiz encouraged Ustinov to invent small bits for his performance, and the results are constantly amusing.

Although We're No Angels doesn't rank with the great Curtiz films, it fits in well with his long parade of holiday features.

The Vagabond King (170)

Next, Curtiz directed The Scarlet Hour (169), a minor western starring Carol Ohmart and Tom Tryon. The less said about his next effort, The Vagabond King (170), the better. The film is a lifeless remake of Rudolf Friml's operetta. Another remake had been done--without the music--in 1930. In 1927, the operetta became a John Barrymore silent, and, in 1938, the famous Ronald Colman vehicle, If I Were King. (The Barrymore film, a lighthearted adventure romp featuring a wonderful performance by the star as well as eye-popping sets and impressive production values, is the most entertaining version, closely followed by the Colman remake.)

The Vagabond King is a tired effort. It suffers from lifeless performances (Leslie Nielsen and Jack Lord, in secondary roles as knights, look like store-window mannequins) and spectacular (but depressingly empty) interior sets, which are made to appear even more desolate when brightly lit by VistaVision photography.

A vulgar production number called "The Life and Times of Mephistopheles" is the last straw. Oreste, an operatic tenor, plays the title role of François Villon with ineffective enthusiasm. Oreste, touted at the time as a major discovery, didn't make it, and neither did the film. Of the many contenders in his extensive film career, The Vagabond King may be Curtiz' worst effort.

The Best Things in Life Are Free (171)

Following a box-office trend is one matter, committing
wretched excess is another. Hollywood pummeled musicals
to near-collapse in the heyday of the '30s. Then it picked
the genre up, brushed it off, and proceeded to pummel it
again during the '50s.

Although Curtiz had creative control over his movies
during his peak Warner Bros. years, and even more so on
his post-Warners films, his direction was often limp and un-
inspired in these pictures. Like many of his contemporaries,
he was apparently hard pressed to find a viable use for the
often extraneous wide-screen/stereo sound/3-D film technology
of the '50s.

Riding the wave of nostalgia that had produced The
Jazz Singer (1953), The Best Things in Life Are Free pays
loud, glittering tribute to three "Tin Pan Alley" song-
writers: Brown, Da Sylva, and Henderson. These collabo-
rators produced flapper music that helped make the '20s
roar, but as film fodder the trio falls flat.

Curtiz, using a tongue-in-cheek approach, aimed for
a Damon Runyon feel. Background figures stumble into the
plot and spout two-dimensional dialogue; they are quickly
forgotten. The director keeps the uneven script rolling,
pausing only for elaborate production numbers and painful
musical interludes. One ludicrous scene reveals the drunken
team throwing a purposeless song together for an irate Al
Jolson. Piqued that the jazz singer would be so insistent,
they write for the star what seems to them to be an embar-
rassingly bad song. The result? Jolson sings the song in,
this, his second sound picture, and he makes it a hit.
Well, that's Hollywood.

Curtiz doesn't lend much life to the overlong and uneven film. Gordon MacRae walks through the movie, and
Ernest Borgnine mugs most of his material. Only dapper
Dan Dailey, an old-time hoofer, stands out; he almost
manages to add a touch of reality to the story. But in the
end, the script, the music, and Curtiz' loose hand sabotage
any such efforts, leaving a colorful, but empty, film.

The Best Things in Life Are Free: Gordon MacRae (left),
Ernest Borgnine, and Dan Dailey.

The Helen Morgan Story (172)

In Hollywood, during almost every decade, the opportunity
comes along to direct a great musical. The Helen Morgan
Story was not such an opportunity.

Singin' in the Rain and the flashy "Gee! Let's put on
a show" gaiety of The Band Wagon had set the pace for '50s
gushing, exuberant musicals. The formula was simple: two-
dimensional characters danced across lavish sets which were
bathed in glowing Technicolor. (Make'em fast, not to last.)
The best of the lot are now regarded as classics. The other
95 percent were long ago cut up into banjo picks.

The Helen Morgan Story stands as the antithesis of
standard musicals of the '50s. Shot in moody black and white,
there's virtually no trace of real happiness anywhere in the
piece. The screenwriters were hard pressed to inject any.

Again, as in the earlier Cole Porter biopic (Night and Day,
1946), actual events (in this case, Helen Morgan's unhappy
life) had to be glossed over. Throughout the film, blues
singer Helen Morgan (Ann Blyth) suffers openly because of
tragic loves. Torn between a good man's (Richard Carlson's)
love for her, and her own love for a bad man (Paul Newman),
she turns to alcohol for comfort. The results are predictable.

Curtiz, near the end of his Warners contract, did little
more with The Helen Morgan Story than watch the progression
of events. Typically, he injects fierce tension into Newman's
scenes with Blyth. But the film falls flat despite the tender
presentation of Morgan's famous torch songs and despite the
curious moments when the director lingers on small reminders
of the period.

It's easy to imagine that the hard-bitten Curtiz is
feeling nostalgic. But, in the cold light of day, the realiza-
tion comes through that he always made movies this way.

●   ●   ●

The Proud Rebel (173) is a nicely done western which stars
Alan Ladd as a Civil War veteran seeking medical help for
his mute son (played by Ladd's real-life son). The film is
understated and never stumbles into obvious sentimental pit-
falls. Also featured in the movie is Olivia de Havilland, who
was reunited with Curtiz at his request.

King Creole (174)

Frank Capra once commented that making a John Wayne movie
was a matter of mixing fast gags and pretty women into a
vehicle where the Duke could play himself. The same formula
held true for Elvis Presley.

Presley was the product of a pop music revolution; he
was a natural screen personality with a built-in audience.
Usually, the quality of the piece he starred in didn't matter.
His enthusiastic fans made all of his movies box-office hits.
After awhile, Presley films became little more than concert
films interrupted by flashes of plot.

In the beginning, though, some effort went into the

production of his vehicles; and King Creole is a prime example
of these efforts.

Presley plays Danny Fisher, a talented singer who falls
under the thumb of mob-boss Walter Matthau. When his career
disrupts his life, Danny tries to make a clean break, but
circumstances line up against him.

This gritty film, shot in grainy black and white, represents a remarkable achievement for the aging Curtiz. Guiding
the primadonna Presley through a solid acting effort, the
director turned out a well-rounded production packed with
typical Curtiz touches. One stand-out sequence takes place
on a surf-pounded beach where the vengeful mobster pursues
the fleeing Presley. Gun-moll Carolyn Jones sacrifices herself for the singer, and the Kid resumes a straight and narrow
life.

Definitely not a typical '50s musical, and certainly not a
typical Elvis Presley feature, King Creole stands on its own
merits as a solid movie, proving that Curtiz' veteran eye had
not lost its sharpness.

•   •   •

Curtiz' next group of films following King Creole included
The Hangman (175), a sluggish western, starring Robert
Taylor and Tina Louise; The Man In the Net (176), a drama
in which Alan Ladd attempts to clear himself of murder;
The Adventures of Huckleberry Finn (177), a sturdy version
of the Twain classic, featuring Tony Randall; A Breath of
Scandal (178), an adaptation of Molnar's play Olympia, which
served as a tepid costume vehicle for Sophia Loren and John
Gavin; and, Francis of Assisi (179), a halfway decent reli-
gious epic, featuring Bradford Dillman in the title role.

At 72, Curtiz was nearing the end of his career and
his life--but he still had one more noteworthy film in him.

The Comancheros (180)

It's only fitting that Michael Curtiz would close out his career
with a rousing action film. Ironically, the aged and ailing
director's participation was limited to mostly interiors; many

of the sprawling action sequences were overseen by second-
unit man Cliff Lyons. Still, the overall look and feel of The
Comancheros bears the unmistakable stamp of the Curtiz design.

John Wayne stood atop the box-office draw scale when
20th Century-Fox set up The Comancheros package. Hollywood never argues with success, so James Edward Grant, a
longtime Wayne friend, collaborated on the screenplay, and
parts were found for Patrick Wayne, as well as for another
old-time crony, Bruce Cabot. Stuart Whitman, riding a wave
of popularity, co-starred with Lee Marvin (in a surprisingly
small role), Ina Balin, and Nehemiah Persoff. Rounding out
the cast were familiar names and faces: Jack Elam, Edgar
Buchanan, Henry Daniell, and Bob Steele.

Somewhere between the tongue-in-cheek giddiness of
North to Alaska and the sparse noir bleakness of The Man
Who Shot Liberty Valance, The Comancheros stands on its
own as a fast-paced western vehicle for John Wayne.

Texas Ranger Jack Cutter (Wayne) tracks down gambler
Paul Regret (Whitman) for killing a man in an illegal duel.
(Curtiz plays the dandified Regret off the rough-hewn Cutter.)
The ranger expresses little regard for his prisoner's powers of
observation, leaving an opening for the gambler to escape
through. In a nicely staged rainstorm, Whitman smashes a
shovel across Wayne's skull and flees. Wayne returns to the
Ranger Station empty-handed, the gentle hazing of his peers
sticking in his throat. He vows to track Regret down. But
his commander throws him a more important mission--to infil-
trate and destroy The Comancheros, an outlaw band supplying
liquor and guns to renegade Indians.

Wayne goes undercover as a gunrunner and, by circum-
stance, is soon thrown together with Regret. Grudgingly,
the two work together, with the clear understanding that
Regret faces arrest when the entire affair is over. The underlying tension of the situation is a familiar Curtiz mark.
Both men grow to respect and even admire each other, but
one is honor-bound to hand the other over for justice. Disguised as gun- and rumrunners, the men gain entrance to the
main stronghold of the Comancheros--a veritable fortress of
a city, built into a canyon with only one access.

The entire operation is lorded over by the Comanchero chieftain--father to Pilar, the woman Regret loves (Balin). Nehemiah Persoff plays the megalomaniacal chieftain, aping just a touch of Robinson's Wolf Larson. Persoff was a familiar T.V. face and was trained in the Broadway theatre. He projects more than enough power to hold sway over his army of cut-throats and leads them and his Indian allies in his quest to rule the entire territory. In one chillingly lit scene, the chieftain torments the captive Cutter by showing him the body of a young ranger (Pat Wayne) who had been sent for help. Left to their own devices, Cutter, Regret, and Pilar try to escape, using Pilar's father as a hostage. The Comancheros follow, and a running battle ensues. When more Indians join the pursuit the odds seem overwhelming, but this scene proves to be the turning point in the action. A company of rangers has been trailing the Indians, and the final battle for the territory begins. Persoff is killed, his forces are scattered, and the rangers triumph. Cutter allows Regret and Pilar to leave, and the matter of honor is closed.

The Comancheros succeeds as popular entertainment. Stripped bare, it offers no pretentions of art, and it doesn't aspire to greater heights than its story intends. What it does offer is professionalism, as well as a solid blend of filmmaking sense.

All in all, that's everything Michael Curtiz wanted to convey in his films.

Michael Curtiz Filmography

1. Ma es Holnap (Today and Tomorrow) - 1912, Hungary.
   Reportedly, Curtiz also co-scripted and acted in this production, the first feature-length film made in Hungary, although this title is unconfirmed.

2. Az Utolsó Bohém (The Last Bohemian) - 1912, Hungary.

3. Rablelek (Captive Soul) - 1913, Hungary.

4. Atlantis - 1913, Denmark.
   Curtiz was an actor in this film, which was directed by August Blom.

5. Unknown Title - 1913, Denmark.
   This film of unknown title was directed by Curtiz and released in 1914 after his return to Hungary.

6. Házasokik Az Uram (My Husband's Getting Married) - 1913, Hungary.

7. Az Ejszaka Rabja (Prisoner of the Night) - 1914, Hungary.
   Curtiz also acted in this film.

8. Aranyásó - 1914, Hungary.

9. Bánk Bán - 1914, Hungary.
   This film was Curtiz' first commercial success as a director; he also acted in it.

10. A Tolonc (The Vagrant) - 1914, Hungary.

11. A Kolesonkert Csecsemok (The Borrowed Babies) - 1914, Hungary.

12. A Hercegnö Pongyolában (The Princess in a Nightrobe) - 1914, Hungary.

13. Akit Ketten Szeretnek (Loved by Two) - 1915, Hungary.
    Curtiz also acted in this film.

14. A Farkas (The Wolf) - 1916, Hungary.

15. A Karthauzi (The Carthusian) - 1916, Hungary.

16. Makkhetes (Seven of Clubs) - 1916, Hungary.

17. A Fekete Szivárvány (The Black Rainbow) - 1916, Hungary.

18. Az Ezust Kecske (The Silver Goat) - 1916, Hungary.

19. Doktor Ur (The Doctor) - 1916, Hungary.

20. A Magyar Föld Ereje (The Strength of the Hungarian Soil) -
    1916, Hungary.

21. A Medikus (The Medic) - 1916, Hungary.
    Curtiz also acted in this film.

22. Zoárd Mester (Master Zoard) - 1917, Hungary.

23. UA Vörös Samson (The Red Samson) - 1917, Hungary.

24. Az Utolsó Hajnal (The Last Dawn) - 1917, Hungary.

25. A Senki Fia (Nobody's Son) - 1917, Hungary.

26. A Szentjóbi Erdó Titka (The Secret of St. Job Forest) - 1917,
    Hungary.

27. A Kuruzsló (The Charlatan) - 1917, Hungary.

28. A Föld Embere (The Man of the Soil) - 1917, Hungary.

29. A Halázcsengö (The Death Bell) - 1917, Hungary.

30. Az Ezredes (The Colonel) - 1917, Hungary.

31. Egy Krajcár Török̈enete (The Story of a Penny) - 1917, Hungary.

32. A Beke Utja (The Road to Peace) - 1917, Hungary.

33. Az Árendás Zsidó (Jean the Tenant) - 1917, Hungary.

34. Tatárjárás (Tartar Invasion) - 1917, Hungary.

35. Az Orvos (The Doctor) - 1917, Hungary.
    This credit is disputed by some sources.

36. Tavasz a Télben (Spring in Winter) - 1918, Hungary.

37. A Napraforgos Holgy (The Lady with Sunflowers) - 1918,
    Hungary.

38. Szamarbor - 1918, Hungary.
    This film is disputed by some sources.

39. Lulu (Lulu) - 1918, Hungary.

40. Kilencven Kilenc (Ninety-nine) - 1918, Hungary.

41. Az Ordog (The Devil) - 1918, Hungary.

42. A Csunya Fiju (The Ugly Boy) - 1918, Hungary.

43. Alraune (The Disguise) - 1918, Hungary.
    Curtiz co-directed this film with Odon Fritz.

44. Judas - 1918, Hungary.

45. A Vig Özvegy (The Merry Widow) - 1918, Hungary.

46. Varázskeringö (Magic Waltz) - 1918, Hungary.

47. Lu, a Kokott (Lu, a Coquette) - 1918, Hungary.

48. Jön Az Öcsem (My Brother is Coming) - 1919, Hungary.

49. A Skorpio - 1919, Hungary.
    This film is unconfirmed, but it may be a Hungarian version
    (completely remade with a Hungarian cast) of part one of Fritz
    Lang's serial Die Spinnen.

50. A Wellington Rejtély (The Wellington Enigma) - 1919, Hungary
    of Sweden.
    This credit is unconfirmed.

51. Liliom - 1919, Hungary.
    Unfinished when Curtiz left Hungary, fleeing the Bela Kun
    regime.

52. Odette et l'Histoire des Femmes Illustrés - 1919, Sweden.
    Supposedly directed by Curtiz after leaving Hungary, and
    said to feature the 14-year old Greta Garbo as Marie Antoinette,
    this film is unconfirmed.

53. Die Dame mit dem Schwarzen Handschuh - 1919, Austria.

54. Der Stern von Damaskus - 1919, Austria.

55. Der Gottesgeissel - 1920, Austria.

56. Die Dame mit den Sonnenblumen - 1920, Austria.

57. Labyrinth des Grauens - 1920, Austria.
    This credit is unconfirmed, and it may be the same film as
    Wege des Schrecken (see entry number 63 on this list).

58. Boccaccio - 1920, Austria.
    This film is unconfirmed.

59. Frau Dorothys Bekenntnis - 1921, Austria.

60. Miss Tutti Frutti - 1921, Austria.

61. Herzogin Satanella - 1921, Austria.
     See entry number 62 on this list.

62. Cherchez la Femme - 1921, Austria.
     This is unconfirmed, and may be the same film as Herzogin
     Satanella (see entry number 61 on this list).

63. Wege des Schrecken - 1921, Austria.
     See entry number 57 on this list.

64. Sodom und Gomorrah: Part One - 1922, Austria.

65. Sodom und Gomorrah: Part Two - 1923, Austria.
     Curtiz is also credited as co-scripter on both parts of this
     film.

66. Samson und Dalila - 1923, Austria.
     This film was directed by Alexander Korda, with Curtiz
     possibly supervising the production.

67. Der Junge Medardus - 1923, Austria.

68. Namenlos - 1923, Austria.

69. Die Lawine - 1923, Austria.
     See entry number 70 on this list.

70. Avalanche - 1924, Austria.
     This is unconfirmed. Some sources claim that this may be
     the same film as Die Lawine (see entry number 69 on this list).

71. Ein Speil Ums Leben - 1924, Austria.

72. General Babka - 1924, Austria.

73. The Uncle from Sumatra - 1924, Austria.

74. Harun al Raschid - 1924, Austria.

75. Die Slavenkönigin - 1924. Austria.
     This film was released in the United States as Moon of Israel.

76. Das Spielzeug von Paris - 1925, Germany-Austria.
     This film was released in the United States as Red Heels.

77. Der Golden Schmetterling - 1926, Germany-Austria.
     This film was released in the United States as The Road to
     Happiness.

78. Flaker Nr. 13 - 1926, Germany-Austria.

                        •   •   •

79. The Third Degree - February, 1926. Warner Bros.-First
     National. Running time: 8 reels.
         Credits - Screenplay: GRAHAM BAKER, adapted from the
     play The Music Master by CHARLES KLEIN. Camera: HAL
     MOHR. Editor: CLARENCE KOLSTER. Assistant Director:
     HENRY BLANKE.
         Cast - JASON ROBARDS, SR. (Howard Jeffries, Jr.),
     DOLORES COSTELLO (Annie Daly), KATE PRICE (Mrs. Chubb),
     LOUISE DRESSER (Alicia Daly), ROCKLIFFE FELLOWES
     (Underwood), with TOM SANTSCHI, HARRY TODD, DAVID
     TORRENCE, MARY LOUISE MILLER, MICHAEL VAVITEN and
     FRED KELSEY.

80. A Million Bid - May, 1927. Warner Bros.-First National.
     Running time: 7 reels.
         Credits - Screenplay: ROBERT DILLON, from a short story
     by GEORGE CAMERON. Camera: HAL MOHR. Assistant
     Director: HENRY BLANKE.
         Cast - DOLORES COSTELLO (Dorothy Gordon), WARNER
     OLAND (Geoff Marsh), MALCOLM McGREGOR (Dr. Robert
     Brent), BETTY BLYTHE (Mrs. Gordon), WILLIAM DEMAREST
     (George Lamont), with DOUGLAS GERRARD and GRACE
     GORDON.

81. The Desired Woman - August, 1927. Warner Bros.-First
     National. Running time: 7 reels.
         Credits - Associate Producer: DARRYL F. ZANUCK.
     Screenplay: ANTHONY COLDEWAY, from a short story by
     MARK CANFIELD. Camera: CONRAD WELLS. Assistant
     Director: HENRY BLANKE.
         Cast - IRENE RICH (Diana Maxwell), WILLIAM RUSSELL
     (Captain Maxwell), WILLIAM COLLIER, JR. (Lieutenant Trent),
     JOHN MILJAN (Lieutenant Kellogg), RICHARD TUCKER
     (Sir Sidney Vincent), with DOUGLAS GERRARD and JOHN
     ACKROYD.

82. Good Time Charley - November, 1927. Warner Bros.-First
     National. Running time: 7 reels.
         Credits - Associate Producer: DARRYL F. ZANUCK.
     Screenplay: ILONA FULOP, adapted by ANTHONY COLDEWAY
     and OWEN FRANCIS from the story The Rainbow Chaser by
     DARRYL F. ZANUCK. Camera: BARNEY McGILL.
         Cast - WARNER OLAND (Good Time Charley), HELENE
     COSTELLO (Rosita Keene), CLYDE COOK (Billy Collins),
     MONTAGU LOVE (John Hartwell), HUGH ALLEN (John Hart-
     well, Jr.), with MARY CARR and JULANNE JOHNSTON.

83. Tenderloin - March, 1928. Warner Bros.-First National.
Running time: 8 reels.
    Credits - Associate Producer: DARRYL F. ZANUCK.
Screenplay: E. T. LOWE, JR., from a story by MELVILLE
CROSMAN. Camera: HAL MOHR. Editor: RALPH DAWSON.
Titles: JOSEPH JACKSON.
    Cast - CONRAD NAGEL (Chuck White), DOLORES COSTELLO
(Rose Shannon), MITCHELL LEWIS (The Professor), DAN
WOLHEIM (Lefty), PAT HARTIGAN (The Mug), with GEORGE
STONE, FRED KELSEY, G. RAYMOND NYE, EVELYN PIERCE,
DOROTHY VERNON and JOHN MILJAN.

84. Noah's Ark - March, 1929. Warner Bros.-First National.
Running time: 75 minutes.
    Credits - Associate Producer: DARRYL F. ZANUCK.
Screenplay: ANTHONY COLDEWAY, from a story by DARRYL
F. ZANUCK. Dialogue: B. LEON ANTHONY. Camera: HAL
MOHR and BARNEY McGILL. Editor: HAROLD McCORD.
Titles: HAROLD McCORD.
    Cast - DOLORES COSTELLO (Mary and Miriam), GEORGE
O'BRIEN (Travis and Japeth), NOAH BEERY, SR. (Nickoloff
and King Nephiliu), LOUISE FAZENDA (Hilda and The Tavern
Maid), GUINN WILLIAMS (Al and Ham), with PAUL McALLISTER,
WILLIAM V. MONG, ANDERS RANDOLF, NIGEL DE BRULIER,
ARMAND KALIZ, MALCOLM WAITE, MYRNA LOY, NOBLE
JOHNSON, OTTO HOFFMAN and JOE BONOMO.

85. The Glad Rag Doll - June, 1929. Warner Bros.-First National.
Running time: 8 reels.
    Credits - Screenplay: GRAHAM BAKER, from a story by
HARVEY GATES. Camera: BYRON HASKIN.
    Cast - DOLORES COSTELLO (Annabel Lee), RALPH GRAVES
(John Fairchild), AUDREY FERRIS (Bertha), ALBERT GRANT
(Nathan Fairchild), MAUDE TURNER GORDON (Aunt Fairchild),
with CLAUDE GILLINGWATER, ARTHUR T. RANKIN, THOMAS
RICKETTS, DALE FULLER, ANDRE BERANGER, DOUGLAS
GERRARD, LEE MORAN, TOM KENNEDY, STANLEY TAYLOR
and LOUISE BEAVERS.

86. Madonna of Avenue A - August, 1929. Warner Bros.-First
National. Running time: 8 reels.
    Credits - Screenplay: RAY DOYLE, from a story by MARK
CANFIELD. Camera: BYRON HASKIN. Editor: RAY DOYLE.
    Cast - DOLORES COSTELLO (Maria), GRANT WITHERS
(Slim), DOUGLAS GERRARD (Arch Duke), LOUISE DRESSER
(Georgia Morton), OTTO HOFFMAN (Monk), with WILLIAM
RUSSELL and LEE MORAN.

87. The Gamblers - August, 1929. Warner Bros.-First National.
Running time: 7 reels.
    Credits - Screenplay: J. GRUBB ALEXANDER, from a story

by CHARLES KLEIN. Camera: WILLIAM REESE. Editor:
THOMAS PRATT.
  Cast - H. B. WARNER (James Darwin), LOIS WILSON
(Catherine Darwin), JASON ROBARDS, SR. (Carvel Emerson),
GEORGE FAWCETT (Emerson, Sr.), JOHNNY ARTHUR (George
Cowper), with FRANK CAMPEAU, PAULINE GARAN and
CHARLES SELLON.

88. Hearts in Exile - November, 1929. Warner Bros.-First
National. Running time: 8 reels.
  Credits - Screenplay: HARVEY GATES, from a story by
JOHN OXENHAM. Camera: BILL REES. Editor: THOMAS
PRATT. Music: HOWARD JACKSON. Titles: B. LEON
ANTHONY.
  Cast - DOLORES COSTELLO (Vera Ivanova), GRANT
WITHERS (Paul Pavloff), JAMES KIRKWOOD (Serge Palma),
DAVID TORRENCE (The Governor), with OLIVE TELL, TOM
DUGAN, GEORGE FAWCETT, WILLIAM IRVING, ROSE DIONE
and CARRIE DAUMERY.

89. Bright Lights - February, 1930. Warner Bros.-First National.
Running time: 73 minutes.
  Credits - Producer: ROBERT NORTH. Screenplay:
HUMPHREY PEARSON, from his own story. Camera: LEE
GARMES. Music: LEO F. FORBSTEIN.
  Cast - DOROTHY MACKAILL (Louanne), FRANK FAY
(Wally Dean), NOAH BEERY, SR. (Miguel Parada), INEZ
COURTNEY (Peggy North), EDDIE NUGENT (Windy Jones),
with DAPHNE POLLARD, EDMUND BREESE, PHILIP STRANGE,
JAMES MURRAY, TOM DUGAN, JEAN BARY, EDWIN LYNCH,
FRANK McHUGH and VIRGINIA SALE.

90. River's End - March, 1930. Warner Bros.-First National.
Running time: 74 minutes.
  Credits - Screenplay: CHARLES KENYON, from a story by
OLIVER CURWOOD. Camera: ROBERT KURRLE. Editor:
RALPH HOLT.
  Cast - CHARLES BICKFORD (Keith and Conniston),
EVELYN KNAPP (Miriam), J. FARRELL MACDONALD (O'Toole),
WALTER MACGRAIL (Martin), ZASU PITTS (Louise), with
DAVID TORRENCE, JUNIOR COUGHLAN and TOM SANTSCHI.

91. Mammy - April, 1930. Warner Bros.-First National. Running
time: 84 minutes.
  Credits - Screenplay: L. G. RIGBY, from the musical
Mr. Bones by IRVING BERLIN, adapted by JOSEPH JACKSON.
Camera: BARNEY McGILL. Music: IRVING BERLIN.
  Cast - AL JOLSON (Al Fuller), LOWELL SHERMAN (Westy),
LOIS MORAN (Nora Meadows), HOBART BOSWORTH (Meadows),
with RAY COOKE, LOUISE DRESSER, TULLY MARSHALL,
MITCHELL LEWIS, STANLEY FIELDS and JACK CURTIS.

92. Under a Texas Moon - April, 1930. Warner Bros.-First
National. Running time: 82 minutes.
    Credits - Screenplay: JOSEPH JACKSON and RAYMOND
GRIFFITH, from the short story Two Gun Man by STEWART
W. WHITE. Camera (Technicolor): WILLIAM REESE. Music:
RAY PERKINS.
    Cast - FRANK FAY (Don Carlos), RAQUEL TORRES
(Raquella), MYRNA LOY (Lita Romero), ARMIDA (Dolores),
NOAH BEERY, SR. (Jed Parker), with GEORGE STONE,
GEORGE COOPER, FRED KOHLER, JACK CURTIS, BETTY
BOYD, CHARLES SELLON, SAM APPEL, EDYTHE KRAMER,
TULLY MARSHALL, MONA MARIS, FRANCISCO MORAN, TOM
DIX, JERRY BARRETT, INEZ GOMEZ and BRUCE COVINGTON.

93. A Soldier's Plaything - May, 1930. Warner Bros.-First
National. Running time: 71 minutes.
    Credits - Screenplay: PERCY VEKROFF, from a story by
VINA DELMAR. Dialogue: ARTHUR CAESAR. Camera:
J. O. TAYLOR. Editor: JACK KILLIFER.
    Cast - HARRY LANGDON (Tim), LOTTI LODER (Gretchen),
BEN LYON (Georgie Wilson), JEAN HERSHOLT (Grandfather
Rittner), NOAH BEERY, SR. (Captain Plover), with FRED
KOHLER, OTTO MATTIESON, LEE MORAN, MARIE ASTAIRE
and FRANK CAMPEAU.

94. The Matrimonial Bed - August, 1930. Warner Bros.-First
National. Running time: 98 minutes.
    Credits - Screenplay: SEYMOUR HICKS and HARVEY THEW,
from a story by YVES MIRANDE and ANDRE MOUEZY-EON.
DEV JENNINGS.
    Cast - LILYAN TASHMAN (Sylvaine), FRANK FAY (Adolphe
Noblet), FLORENCE ELDREDGE (Juliette Corton), JAMES
GLEASON (Gustave Corton), BERYL MERCER (Corinne), with
VIVIAN OAKLAND, ARTHUR EDMUND CAREWE, MARION
BYRON and JAMES BRADBURY, SR.

95. Daemon des Meeres - August, 1930. Warner Bros.-First
National. Running time: 75 minutes.
    Credits - Screenplay: OLIVER H. P. GARRETT and ULRICH
STEINDORFF, adapted from the novel Moby Dick by HERMAN
MELVILLE. Camera: ROBERT KURRLE.
    Cast - WILLIAM DIETERLE (Captain Ahab), with ANTON
POINTER, KARL ELTINGER, LISZLY ARNA, CARLA BARTHEEL
and LOTHAR MAYRONG.
Note - This film is a German-language version of the same
studio's Moby Dick (directed by Lloyd Bacon, starring John
Barrymore and Joan Bennett), completely refilmed with a
German-speaking cast, and was shot simultaneously with the
domestic version directed by Bacon.

96. God's Gift to Women - April, 1931. Warner Bros.-First National.

Running time: 71 minutes.
Credits - Screenplay: JOSEPH JACKSON and RAYMOND
GRIFFITH, adapted from the play The Devil Was Sick by JANE
HINTON. Camera: ROBERT KURRLE. Editor: JAMES
GRIBBON.
Cast - JOAN BLONDELL, FRANK FAY, LAURA LaPLANTE,
ARTHUR EDMUND CAREWE, CHARLES WINNINGER, ALAN
MOWBRAY, CHARLES JUDELS, TYRELL DAVIS, LOUISE
BROOKS, BILLY HOUSE and YOLA D'AVRIL.

97. The Mad Genius - October, 1931. Warner Bros.-First National.
Running time: 81 minutes.
Credits - Screenplay: J. G. ALEXANDER and HARVEY
THEW, adapted from the play The Idol by MARTIN BROWN.
Camera: BARNEY McGILL. Art Director: ANTON GROT.
Editor: RALPH DAWSON. Ballet Choreography: ADOLPH
BOLM.
Cast - JOHN BARRYMORE (Tsarakov), MARIAN MARSH
(Nana), DONALD COOK (Fedor), CARMEL MYERS (Preskoya),
CHARLES BUTTERWORTH (Karminsky), with LUIS ALBERNI,
ANDRE LUGET, BORIS KARLOFF, FRANKIE DARRO and MAE
MADISON.

98. The Woman from Monte Carlo - January, 1932. Warner Bros.-
First National. Running time: 68 minutes.
Credits - Screenplay: HARVEY THEW, from a story by
CLAUDE FERRERE and LUCIEN NAPOTHY. Camera: ERNEST
HALLER. Editor: HAROLD McLERNON.
Cast - LIL DAGOVER (Lottie), WALTER HUSTON (Captain
Corlaix), WARREN WILLIAM (D'Ortelles), JOHN WRAY
(Brambourg), ROBERT WARWICK (Morbraz), with BEN
HENDRICKS, GEORGE E. STONE, MATT McHUGH, MAUDE
EBURNE, DEWEY ROBINSON, ROBERT ROSE, REGINALD
BARLOW, CLARENCE MUSE, FREDERICK BURTON, OSCAR
APFEL, JOHN RUTHERFORD, FRANCIS McDONALD, WARNER
RICHMOND, FRANK LEIGH, PAUL PORCASI, JACK KENNEDY
and ELINOR WESSELHOEFT.

99. Alias the Doctor - March, 1932. Warner Bros. - First National.
Running time: 69 minutes.
Credits - Co-Director: LLOYD BACON. Screenplay:
HOUSTON BRANCH and CHARLES KENYON, from a play by
CHARLES FOELDES. Camera: BARNEY McGILL. Editor:
WILLIAM HOLMES.
Cast - RICHARD BARTHELMESS (Karl Muller), MARIAN
MARSH (Lotti), LUCILLE LaVERNE (Mother Brenner), NORMAN
FOSTER (Stephen), ADRIENNE DOR (Anna), with OSCAR
APFEL, JOHN ST. POLIS, WALLIS CLARK, GEORGE ROSENER,
REGINALD BARLOW, ARNOLD LUCY, HAROLD WALDRIDGE,
ROBERT FARFAN and BORIS KARLOFF.

100. The Strange Love of Molly Louvain - May, 1932. Warner Bros.-
      First Naitonal. Running time: 70 minutes.
          Credits - Screenplay: ERWIN GELSEY and BROWN HOLMES,
      adapted from the play Tinsel Girl by MAURICE WATKINS.
      Camera: ROBERT KURRLE. Editor: JAMES BORBY.
          Cast - ANN DVORAK (Molly), LEE TRACY (Scotty),
      RICHARD CROMWELL (Jimmy), GUY KIBBEE (Pop), LESLIE
      FENTON (Nick), with FRANK McHUGH, CHARLES MIDDLETON,
      EVELYN KNAPP, HANK MANN, C. HENRY GORDON, MARY
      DORAN, HARRY BERESFORD, HAROLD WALDRIDGE, WILLIAM
      BURESS, WILLARD ROBERTSON, CLAIRE McDOWELL, MAURICE
      BLACK, BEN ALEXANDER, RICHARD CRAMER and DONALD
      DILLAWAY.

101. Doctor X - August, 1932. Warner Bros.-First National.
      Running time: 80 minutes.
          Credits - Executive Producer: HAL B. WALLIS. Screen-
      play: EARL BALDWIN and ROBERT TASKER, adapted from
      the play by HOWARD W. COMSTOCK and ALLEN C. MILLER.
      Camera (Technicolor): RAY RENNAHAN and RICHARD
      TOWER. Art Director: ANTON GROT. Editor: GEORGE
      AMY. Makeup: MAX FACTOR. Music: LEO F. FORBSTEIN.
          Cast - LIONEL ATWILL (Doctor Xavier), FAY WRAY (Joan
      Xavier), LEE TRACY (Lee), PRESTON FOSTER (Doctor
      Welles), with ARTHUR EDMUND CAREWE, JOHN WRAY,
      GEORGE ROSENER, LEILA BENNETT, HARRY BERESFORD,
      MAE BUSCH, TOM DUGAN, ROBERT WARWICK, THOMAS
      JACKSON, WILLARD ROBERTSON and HARRY HOLMAN.

102. Cabin in the Cotton - September, 1932. Warner Bros.-First
      National. Running time: 77 minutes.
          Credits - Executive Producer: JACK L. WARNER. Co-
      Director: WILLIAM KEIGHLEY. Screenplay: PAUL GREEN,
      based on the novel by HARRY HARRISON KROLL. Camera:
      BARNEY McGILL. Editor: GEORGE AMY.
          Cast - BETTE DAVIS (Madge), RICHARD BARTHELMESS
      (Marvin), DOROTHY JORDAN (Betty), HENRY B. WALTHALL
      (Old Eph), BERTON CHURCHILL (Lane Norwood), with
      WALTER PERCIVAL, WILLIAM LeMAIRE, TULLY MARSHALL,
      EDMUND BREESE, CLARENCE MUSE, JOHN MARSTON,
      RUSSELL SIMPSON, ERVILLE ANDERSON, DOROTHY PETER-
      SON, SNOWFLAKE (FRED TOOMES), HARRY CORDING,
      TREVOR BARDETTE, VIRGINIA HAMMOND, CHARLES KING,
      FLORINE McKINNEY, DAVID LANDAU, DENNIS O'KEEFE
      and J. CARROL NAISH.

103. 20,000 Years in Sing Sing - January, 1933. Warner Bros.-
      First National. Running time: 81 minutes.
          Credits - Producer: ROBERT LORD. Screenplay: WILSON
      MIZNER and BROWN HOLMES, adapted by COURTNEY TERRALL
      and ROBERT LORD from the novel by LEWIS E. LAWES.

Camera: BARNEY McGILL. Art Director: ANTON GROT.
Editor: GEORGE AMY. Music: BERNHARD KAUN.
  Cast - SPENCER TRACY (Tom Connors), BETTE DAVIS
(Fay), LYLE TALBOT (Bud), SHEILA TERRY (Billie),
LOUIS CALHERN (Joe Finn), ARTHUR BYRON (Warden
Long), with WARREN HYMER, EDWARD McNAMARA, SPENCER
CHARTERS, SAM GODFREY, HAROLD HUBER, GRANT
MITCHELL, NELLA WALKER, ARTHUR HOYT, WILLIAM
LeMAIRE and GEORGE PAT COLLINS.

104. Mystery of the Wax Museum - February, 1933. Warner Bros.-
First National. Running time: 77 minutes.
  Credits - Producer: HENRY BLANKE. Screenplay: DON
MULLALY and CARL ERICKSON, from a story by CHARLES
S. BELDEN. Camera (Technicolor): RAY RENNAHAN.
Art Director: ANTON GROT. Editor: GEORGE AMY.
Makeup: PERC WESTMORE. Wax Sculptures: L. E. OTIS
and H. CLAY CAMPBELL. Music: Leo F. Forbstein.
  Cast - LIONEL ATWILL (Ivan Igor), FAY WRAY (Charlotte
Duncan), GLENDA FARRELL (Florence), FRANK McHUGH
(Jim), ALLEN VINCENT (Ralph Burton), GAVIN GORDON
(George Winton), EDWIN MAXWELL (Joe Worth), HOLMES
HERBERT (Doctor Rasmussen), CLAUDE KING (Golatily),
ARTHUR EDMUND CAREWE (Sparrow), THOMAS JACKSON
(Detective), DeWITT JENNINGS (Police Captain), MATTHEW
BETZ (Otto), BULL ANDERSON (Janitor), PAT O'MALLEY
(Plain-clothes Man), MONICA BANNISTER (Joan Gale).

105. The Keyhole - March, 1933. Warner Bros.-First National.
Running time: 66 minutes.
  Credits - Screenplay: ROBERT PRESNELL, based on the
short story Adventuress by ALICE DUER MILLER. Dialogue:
ARTHUR GREVILLE COLLINS. Camera: BARNEY McGILL.
  Cast - KAY FRANCIS (Anne Brooks), GEORGE BRENT
(Neil Davis), GLENDA FARRELL (Dot), ALLEN JENKINS
(Hank Wales), MONROE OWSLEY (Brooks), with HELEN WARE
and HENRY KOLKER.

106. Private Detective 62 (Reissue Title: MAN KILLER) - July,
1933. Warner Bros.-First National. Running time: 67
minutes.
  Credits - Screenplay: RIAN JAMES, based on a short
story by RAOUL WHITFIELD. Camera: TONY GAUDIO. Art
Director: JACK OKEY.
  Cast - WILLIAM POWELL (Donald Free), MARGARET
LINDSAY (Janet), RUTH DONNELLY (Amy), GORDON WEST-
COTT (Bandor), JAMES BELL (Whitey), with ARTHUR BYRON,
NATHALIE MOOREHEAD, THERESA HARRIS, SHEILA TERRY,
RENEE WHITNEY, ANN HOVEY, IRVING BACON, ARTHUR
HOHL and HOBART CAVANAUGH.

107. Goodbye Again - September, 1933. Warner Bros.-First
      National. Running time: 65 minutes.
          Credits - Screenplay: BEN MARKSON, from a story by
      GEORGE HAIGHT and ALLAN SCOTT. Camera: GEORGE
      BARNES. Editor: THOMAS PRATT.
          Cast - WARREN WILLIAM (Kenneth Bixby), JOAN BLONDELL
      (Anne), GENEVIEVE TOBIN (Julie Wilson), HELEN CHANDLER
      (Elizabeth), with WALLACE FORD, HOBART CAVANAUGH,
      HUGH HERBERT, JAY WARD, RAY COOKE, RUTH DONNELLY
      and FERDINAND GOTTSCHALK.

108. The Kennel Murder Case - October, 1933. Warner Bros.-First
      National. Running time: 73 minutes.
          Credits - Producer: ROBERT PRESNELL. Screenplay:
      ROBERT N. LEE and PETER MILNE, from a story by S. S.
      VAN DINE. Camera: WILLIAM REESE. Art Director: JACK
      OKEY. Editor: HAROLD McLARNIN.
          Cast - WILLIAM POWELL (Philo Vance), MARY ASTOR
      (Hilda Lake), EUGENE PALLETTE (Heath), RALPH MORGAN
      (Raymond Wrede), HELEN VINSON (Doris Delafield),
      ETIENNE GIRARDOT (Doremud), with PAUL CAVANAUGH,
      ROBERT BARRAT, JACK La RUE, ARTHUR HOHL, ROBERT
      McWADE, HENRY O'NEILL, FRANK CONROY, SPENCER
      CHARTERS, JAMES LEE and CHARLES WILSON.

109. Female - November, 1933. Warner Bros.-First National.
      Running time: 60 minutes.
          Credits - Producer: HENRY BLANKE. Co-Director:
      WILLIAM DIETERLE. Screenplay: GENE MARKEY and
      KATHRYN SCOLA, based on the novel by DONALD HENDERSON
      CLARK. Camera: SID HICKOX. Art Director: JACK OKEY.
      Editor: JACK KILLIFER.
          Cast - RUTH CHATTERTON (Nancy), GEORGE BRENT (Jim
      Thorne), PHILIP FAVERSHAM (Claybourne), RUTH DONNELLY
      (Miss Frothingham), JOHNNY MACK BROWN (Cooper), with
      FERDINAND GOTTSCHALK, PHILIP REED, LOIS WILSON,
      HUEY WHITE, ERIC WILTON, WALTER WALKER, RAFAELO
      OTTIANO, CHARLES WILSON, KENNETH THOMPSON, EDWARD
      COOPER, DOUGLAS DUMBRILLE, SAMUEL S. HINDS,
      STERLING HOLLOWAY, USAY O'DAVERN, SPENCER CHARTERS,
      ROBERT GREIG, LAURA HOPE CREWS, ROBERT WARWICK and
      GAVIN GORDON.

110. Mandalay - February, 1934. Warner Bros.-First National.
      Running time: 65 minutes.
          Credits - Associate Producer: ROBERT PRESNELL. Screen-
      play: AUSTIN PARKER and CHARLES KENYON, based on a
      short story by PAUL HERVEY FOX. Camera: TONY GAUDIO.
      Art Director: ANTON GROT. Editor: THOMAS PRATT.
          Cast - KAY FRANCIS (Tanya), RICARDO CORTEZ (Tony
      Evans), WARNER OLAND (Nick), LYLE TALBOT (Doctor Greg

Barton), RUTH DONNELLY (Mrs. Peters), SHIRLEY TEMPLE
(Betty Shaw), with REGINALD OWEN, RAFAELA OTTIANO,
DAVID TORRENCE, HALLIWELL HOBBES, ETIENNE
GIRARDOT, LUCIEN LITTLEFIELD, HERMAN BING, BODIL
ROSING, HOBART CAVANAUGH, JAMES B. LEONG, HARRY
C. BRADLEY, LILLIAN HARMER and TORBEN MEYER.

111. Jimmy the Gent - March, 1934. Warner Bros.-First National.
Running time: 67 minutes.
    Credits - Executive Producer: JACK L. WARNER.
Screenplay: BERTRAM MILHAUSER, from the story The Heir
Chaser by LAIRD DOYLE and RAY NAZARRO. Camera: IRA
MORGAN. Art Director: ESDRAS HARTLEY. Editor:
THOMAS RICHARDS. Music: LEO F. FORBSTEIN.
    Cast - JAMES CAGNEY (Jimmy Corrigan), BETTE DAVIS
(Joan Martin), ALICE WHITE (Mabel), ALLEN JENKINS
(Louie), ARTHUR HOHL (Joe Rector and Monty Barton),
ALAN DINEHART (James J. Wallingham), PHILIP REED (Ronnie
Gatston), HOBART CAVANAUGH (The Imposter), MAYO
METHOT (Gladys Farrell), RALF HAROLDE (Hendrickson),
JOSEPH SAWYER (Mike), PHILIP FAVERSHAM (Blair), NORA
LANE (Posy Barton), with JOSEPH CREHAN, ROBERT
WARWICK, MERNA KENNEDY, RENEE WHITNEY, MONICA
BANNISTER, DON DOUGLAS, BUD FLANAGAN, LEONARD
MUDIE, HARRY HOLMAN, CAMILLE ROVELLE, STANLEY
MACK, TOM COSTELLO, BEN HENDRICKS, BILLY WEST,
EDDIE SHUBERT, LEE MORAN, HARRY WALLACE, ROBERT
HOMANS, MILTON KIBBEE, HOWARD HICKMAN, EULA GUY,
JULIET WARE, RICKEY NEWELL, LORENA LAYSON, DICK
FRENCH and JAY EATON.

112. The Key (Reissue Title: High Peril) - May, 1934. Warner
Bros.-First National. Running time: 72 minutes.
    Credits - Producer: ROBERT PRESNELL. Screenplay:
LAIRD DOYLE, based on a play by R. GORE BROWNE and
J. L. HARDY. Camera: ERNEST HALLER. Art Director:
ROBERT HAAS. Editors: WILLIAM CLEMENS and THOMAS
RICHARDS.
    Cast - EDNA BEST (Nora), WILLIAM POWELL (Captain
Jennant), COLIN CLIVE (Andrew Kerr), MAXINE DOYLE
(Pauline), DONALD CRISP (Conlan), with HOBART
CAVANAUGH, HALLIWELL HOBBES, PHIL REGAN, ARTHUR
TREACHER, ARTHUR AYLESWORTH, ANNE SHIRLEY,
HENRY O'NEILL, GERTRUDE SHORT and J. M. KERRIGAN.

113. British Agent - September, 1934. Warner Bros.-First
National. Running time: 81 minutes.
    Credits - Producer: HENRY BLANKE. Associate Producer:
ROBERT PRESNELL. Screenplay: LAIRD DOYLE, based on
the memoirs of BRUCE LOCKHART. Camera: ERNEST HALLER.
Art Director: ANTON GROT. Editor: THOMAS RICHARDS.

Music: LEO F. FORBSTEIN.
    Cast - LESLIE HOWARD (Stephen Locke), KAY FRANCIS
(Elena), IRVING PICHEL (Stalin), J. CARROL NAISH
(Trotsky), WILLIAM GARGAN (Medill), PHILIP REED (Le
Farge), with IVAN SIMPSON, WALTER BYRON, CESAR
ROMERO, ARTHUR AYLESWORTH, HALLIWELL HOBBES,
ALPHONSE ETHIER, TENEN HOLT, DORIS LLOYD, MARINA
SHUBERT, GEORGE PEARCE, GREGORY GAYE, PAUL
PORCASI, ADDISON RICHARDS and WALTER ARMITAGE.

114. Black Fury - April, 1935. Warner Bros.-First National.
      Running time: 92 minutes.
          Credits - Producer: ROBERT LORD. Screenplay: ABEM
      FINKEL and CARL ERICKSON, adapted from the story Jan
      Volkanik by JUDGE M. A. MUSSMANO and the play Bohunk
      by HARRY R. IRVING. Camera: BYRON HASKIN. Art
      Director: JOHN J. HUGHES. Editor: THOMAS RICHARDS.
          Cast - PAUL MUNI (Joe Radek), WILLIAM GARGAN (Slim
      Johnson), TULLY MARSHALL (Tommy Poole), KAREN MORLEY
      (Anna Novak), MAE MARSH (Mary Novak), with BARTON
      MacLANE, JOHN QUALEN, J. CARROL NAISH, VINCE
      BARNETT, WADE BOTELER, HENRY O'NEILL, EFFIE ELLS-
      LER, WILLARD ROBERTSON, EGON BRECHER, GEORGE PAT
      COLLINS, WARD BOND, JOSEPH CREHAN, AKIM TAMIROFF,
      PURNELL PRATT, EDDIE SHUBERT, SARA HADEN, PAT
      MORIARTY, SELMAR JACKSON, EDITH FELLOWS, JUNE
      EBBERLING, BOBBY NELSON, DOROTHY GRAY, JACK
      BLEIFER, GEORGE OFFERMAN, JR., FLOYD SHACKELFORD,
      WALLY ALBRIGHT, MICKEY RENTSCHLER and PEDRO
      REGAN.

115. The Case of the Curious Bride - April, 1935. Warner Bros.-
      First National. Running time: 80 minutes.
          Credits - Producer: HARRY JOE BROWN. Screenplay:
      TOM REED and BROWN HOLMES, based on a novel by ERLE
      STANLEY GARDNER. Camera: DAVID ABEL. Art Directors:
      CARL JULES WEYL and ANTON GROT. Editor: TERRY
      MORSE. Music: BERNARD KAUN.
          Cast - WARREN WILLIAM (Perry Mason), MARGARET
      LINDSAY (Rhoda Montaine), DONALD WOODS (Carl Montaine),
      CLAIRE DODD (Della Street), ALLEN JENKINS (Spudsy),
      PHILIP REED (Doctor Claude Millbeck), BARTON MacLANE
      (Joe Lucas), WINIFRED SHAW (Doris Pender), WARREN HYMER
      (Oscar Pender), OLIN HOWLAND (Coroner Wilbur Strong),
      CHARLES RICHMAN (G. Phillip Montaine), THOMAS JACKSON
      (Toots Howard), ERROL FLYNN (Gregory Moxley) with
      ROBERT GLECKLER, JAMES DONLAN, MAYO METHOT,
      GEORGE HUMBERT, HENRY KOLKER and PAUL HURST.

116. Front Page Woman - July, 1935. Warner Bros.-First National.
      Running time: 82 minutes.

Credits - Producer: SAMUEL BISCHOFF. Screenplay: LAIRD DOYLE, ROY CHANSLOR and LILLIE HAYWARD, adapted from the story Women Are Born Newspapermen by RICHARD MACAULEY. Camera: TONY GAUDIO. Art Director: JOHN HUGHES. Editor: TERRY MORSE. Music: HEINZ ROEMHELD.

Cast - BETTE DAVIS (Ellen), GEORGE BRENT (Curt), JUNE MARTEL (Olive), JOSEPH CREHAN (Spike), ROSCOE KARNS (Toots), with DOROTHY DARE, WINIFRED SHAW, J. CARROL NAISH, JOSEPH KING, WALTER WALKER, J. FARRELL MacDONALD, De WITT JENNINGS, GRACE HALE, HUNTLEY GORDON, ADRIAN ROSLEY, GEORGE RENAVENT, GORDON WESTCOTT, SELMAR JACKSON, ADDISON RICHARDS and MIKE MONK.

117. Little Big Shot - November, 1935. Warner Bros.-First National. Running time: 78 minutes.

Credits - Producer: SAMUEL BISCHOFF. Screenplay: JERRY WALD, JULIUS J. EPSTEIN and ROBERT ANDREWS, from a story by HARRISON JACOBS. Camera: TONY GAUDIO. Art Director: HUGH RETTICHER. Editor: JACK KILLIFER. Music: LEO FORBSTEIN.

Cast - SYBIL JASON (Gloria Gibbs), GLENDA FARRELL (Jean), ROBERT ARMSTRONG (Steve Craig), EDWARD EVERETT HORTON (Mortimer Thompson) with EDGAR KENNEDY, JACK La RUE, MARY FOY, ARTHUR VINTON, ADDISON RICHARDS, JOSEPH SAWYER, TAMMANY YOUNG, EMMA DUNN, WARD BOND, GUY USHER, MURRAY ALPER and MARC LAWRENCE.

118. Captain Blood - December, 1935. Warner Bros.-First National. Running time: 99 minutes.

Credits - Producer: HAL B. WALLIS. Associate Producers: HARRY JOE BROWN and GORDON HOLLINGSHEAD. Screenplay: CASEY ROBINSON, based on the novel by RAFAEL SABATINI. Camera: HAL MOHR. Additional Photography: ERNEST HALLER. Art Director: ANTON GROT. Music: ERICH WOLFGANG KORNGOLD. Orchestrations: HUGO FRIEDHOFER. Editor: GEORGE AMY. Special Effects: FRED JACKMAN. Sound: C. A. RIGGS. Fencing Master: FRED CAVENS. Gowns: MILO ANDERSON. Assistant Director: SHERRY SHOURDS. Dialogue Director: STANLEY LOGAN.

Cast - ERROL FLYNN (Peter Blood), OLIVIA de HAVILLAND (Arabella Bishop), LIONEL ATWILL (Colonel Bishop), BASIL RATHBONE (Captain Levasseur), ROSS ALEXANDER (Jeremy Pitt), GUY KIBBEE (Hagthorpe), HENRY STEPHENSON (Lord Willoughby), ROBERT BARRAT (Wolverstone), HOBART CAVANAUGH (Doctor Bronson), DONALD MEEK (Doctor Whacker), JESSIE RALPH (Mrs. Barlowe), FORRESTER HARVEY (Honesty Nuttall), FRANK McGLYNN, Sr. (Reverend Ogle),

HOLMES HERBERT (Captain Gardner), DAVID TORRENCE
(Andrew Baynes), J. CARROL NAISH (Cahusac), PEDRO De
CORDOBA (Don Diego), GEORGE HASSELL (Governor Steed),
HARRY CORDING (Kent), LEONARD MUDIE (Baron Jeffreys),
IVAN SIMPSON (Prosecutor), STUART CASEY (Captain
Hobart), DENIS D'AUBURN (Lord Gildoy), MARY FORBES
(Mrs. Steed), E. E. CLIVE (Court Clerk), COLIN KENNY
(Lord Chester Dyke), MAUDE LESLIE (Mrs. Baynes),
GARDNER JAMES (Branded Slave) and VERNON STEELE
(King James).

119. Stolen Holiday - February, 1936. Warner Bros.-First National.
Running time: 84 minutes.
     Credits - Producer: HAL B. WALLIS. Associate Producer:
HARRY JOE BROWN. Screenplay: CASEY ROBINSON, from a
story by WARREN DUFF and VIRGINIA KELLOGG. Camera:
SID HICKOX. Art Director: ANTON GROT. Editor: TERRY
MORSE. Music: LEO FORBSTEIN.
     Cast - KAY FRANCIS (Nicole Picot), CLAUDE RAINS
(Stefan Orloff), IAN HUNTER (Anthony Wayne), ALISON
SKIPWORTH (Suzanne), ALEXANDER D'ARCY (Anatole) with
WALTER KINGSFORD, BETTY LAWFORD, CHARLES HALTON,
EGON BRECHER, FRANK REICHER, ROBERT STRANGE, FRANK
CONROY, WEDGEWOOD HOWELL and KATHLEEN HOWARD.

120. The Walking Dead - March, 1936. Warner Bros.-First National.
Running time: 66 minutes.
     Credits - Screenplay: EWART ADAMSON, PETER MILNE,
ROBERT ADAMS and LILLIE HAYWARD. Camera: HAL MOHR.
Editor: THOMAS PRATT. Makeup: PERC WESTMORE.
     Cast - BORIS KARLOFF (John Ellman), RICARDO CORTEZ
(Nolan), MARGUERITE CHURCHILL (Nancy), EDMUND GWENN
(Doctor Beaumont), WARREN HULL (Jimmy) with BARTON
MacLANE, HENRY O'NEILL, ADDISON HEHR, MIKE MORITA,
RUTH ROBINSON, KENNETH HARLAN, EDDIE ACUFF, JOE
SAWYER, ADRIAN ROSLEY, JOSEPH KING, PAUL HARVEY,
ADDISON RICHARDS and ROBERT STRANGE.

121. The Charge of the Light Brigade - November, 1936. Warner
Bros.-First National. Running time: 116 minutes.
     Credits - Producer: HAL B. WALLIS. Associate Producer:
SAMUEL BISCHOFF. Screenplay: MICHAEL JACOBY and
ROWLAND LEIGH, based on an original story by MICHAEL
JACOBY and the poem by ALFRED TENNYSON. Camera:
SOL POLITO. Art Director: JOHN HUGHES. Music: MAX
STEINER. Orchestrations: HUGO FRIEDHOFER. Editor:
GEORGE AMY. Second-unit Director: B. REEVES EASON.
Special Effects: FRED JACKMAN and H. F. KOENEKAMP.
Sound: C. A. RIGGS. Assistant Director: JACK SULLIVAN.
Dialogue Director: STANLEY LOGAN. Technical Advisor:
MAJOR SAM HARRIS. Gowns: MILO ANDERSON.

Cast - ERROL FLYNN (Major Geoffrey Vickers), OLIVIA
de HAVILLAND (Elsa Campbell), PATRICK KNOWLES (Captain
Perry Vickers), HENRY STEPHENSON (Sir Charles Macefield),
NIGEL BRUCE (Sir Benjamin Warrenton), DONALD CRISP
(Colonel Campbell), DAVID NIVEN (Captain Randall), C.
HENRY GORDON (Surat Khan), G. P. HUNTLEY, JR. (Major
Jowett), ROBERT BARRAT (Count Igor Volonoff), SPRING
BYINGTON (Lady Octavia Warrenton), E. E. CLIVE (Sir
Humphrey Harcourt), J. CARROL NAISH (Subahdar-Major
Puran Singh), WALTER HOLBROOK (Cornet Barclay),
CHARLES SEDGWICK (Cornet Pearson), SCOTTY BECKETT
(Prema Singh), LUMSDEN HARE (Colonel Woodward),
PRINCESS BAIGUM (Prema's Mother), GEORGE REGAS
(Wazir), COLIN KENNY (Major Anderson), GORDON HART
(Colonel Coventry), HELEN SANBORN (Mrs. Jowett), HOLMES
HERBERT (General O'Neill), BOYD IRWIN (General Dunbar),
REGINALD SHEFFIELD (Bentham), GEORGES RENAVENT
(General Canrobert), CHARLES CROKER KING (Lord Cardigan)
and BRANDON HURST (Lord Raglan).

122. Kid Galahad (Reissue title: The Battling Bellhop) - May,
      1937. Warner Bros.-First National. Running time: 101
      minutes.
          Credits - Producer: HAL B. WALLIS. Screenplay: SETON
      I. MILLER, based on the novel by FRANCIS WALLACE.
      Camera: TONY GAUDIO. Art Director: CARL JULES WEYL.
      Editor: GEORGE AMY. Music: HEINZ ROEMHELD and MAX
      STEINER.
          Cast - WAYNE MORRIS (Ward Guisenberry), EDWARD G.
      ROBINSON (Nick Donati), BETTE DAVIS (Fluff), HUMPHREY
      BOGART (Turkey Morgan), JANE BRYAN (Marie), HARRY
      CAREY (Silver Jackson) with SOLEDAD JIMINEZ, WILLIAM
      HAADE, VEDA ANN BORG, BEN WELDEN, JOSEPH CREHAN,
      HARLAND TUCKER, HORACE MacMAHON, JOYCE COMPTON,
      FRANK FAYLEM, HANK HANKINSON, BOB EVANS, JACK
      KRANZ, BOB NESTELL, GEORGE BLAKE and JOE CUNNING-
      HAM.

123. Mountain Justice - May, 1937. Warner Bros.-First National.
      Running time: 83 minutes.
          Credits - Screenplay: NORMAN REILLY RAINE and LUCI
      WARD, based on their original story. Camera: ERNEST
      HALLER. Art Director: MAX PARKER. Editor: GEORGE
      AMY.
          Cast - JOSEPHINE HUTCHINSON (Ruth Harkins), GUY
      KIBBEE (Doc Barnard), GEORGE BRENT (Paul Cameron),
      ROBERT McWADE (Horace Bamber), ROBERT BARRAT (Jeff
      Hawkins), MONA BARRIE (Evelyn Wayne), EDWIN PAWLEY
      (Tod Miller) with MARGARET HAMILTON, FUZZY KNIGHT,
      ELIZABETH RISDON, MARCIA MAE JONES, GRANVILLE BATES,
      SIBYL HARRISON, RUSSELL SIMPSON and GUY WILKERSON.

124. The Perfect Specimen - October, 1937. Warner Bros.-First
      National. Running time: 97 minutes.
          Credits - Producer: HAL B. WALLIS. Associate Producer:
      HARRY JOE BROWN. Screenplay: NORMAN REILLY RAINE,
      LAWRENCE RILEY and BREWSTER MORSE, based on a story
      by SAMUEL HOPKINS ADAMS. Camera: CHARLES ROSHER.
      Art Director: ROBERT HAAS. Editor: TERRY MORSE.
      Music: HEINZ ROEMHELD. Sound: EVERETT A. BROWN.
          Cast - ERROL FLYNN (Gerald Beresford), JOAN BLONDELL
      (Mona Carter), HUGH HERBERT (Kiiligrew Shaw), EDWARD
      EVERETT HORTON (Mr. Grattan), DICK FORAN (Jink Carter),
      BEVERLY ROBERTS (Alicia), MAY ROBSON (Mrs. Leona
      Wicks), ALLEN JENKINS (Pinky), DENNIE MOORE (Clarabelle),
      HUGH O'CONNELL (Hotel Clerk), JAMES BURKE (Snodgrass),
      GRANVILLE BATES (Hooker), HARRY DAVENPORT (Carl
      Carter), TIM HENNING (Briggs), and SPENCER CHARTERS.

125. Gold Is Where You Find It - February, 1938. Warner Bros.-
      First National. Running time: 90 minutes.
          Credits - Producer: HAL B. WALLIS. Screenplay:
      WARREN DUFF and ROBERT BUCKNER, from a story by
      CLEMENTS RIPLEY. Camera (Technicolor): SOL POLITO.
      Special Effects: BYRON HASKIN. Art Director: TED
      SMITH. Editor: CLARENCE KOLSTER. Music: MAX
      STEINER.
          Cast - GEORGE BRENT (Jared Whitney), OLIVIA de
      HAVILLAND (Serena Ferris), CLAUDE RAINS (Colonel Ferris),
      MARGARET LINDSAY (Rosanne), JOHN LITEL (Ralph Ferris)
      with MARCIA RALSTON, BARTON MacLANE, TIM HOLT,
      SIDNEY TOLER, HENRY O'NEILL, WILLIE BEST, ROBERT
      McWADE, GEORGE HAYES, RUSSELL SIMPSON, CLARENCE
      KOLB, HARRY DAVENPORT, GRANVILLE BATES, MORONI
      OLSEN, ROBERT HOMANS and EDDIE CHANDLER.

126. The Adventures of Robin Hood - May, 1938. Warner Bros.-
      First National. Running time: 102 minutes.
          Credits - Producer: HAL B. WALLIS. Associate Producer:
      HENRY BLANKE. Co-Director: WILLIAM KEIGHLEY. Screen-
      play: NORMAN REILLY RAINE and SETON I. MILLER.
      Camera (Technicolor): TONY GAUDIO and SOL POLITO.
      Technicolor Color Director: NATALIE KALMUS. Assistant:
      MORGAN PADELFORD. Art Director: CARL JULES WEYL.
      Music: ERICH WOLFGANG KORNGOLD. Orchestrations:
      HUGO FRIEDHOFER and MILAN RODER. Music Director: LEO
      FORBSTEIN. Editor: RALPH DAWSON. Second-unit Director:
      B. REEVES EASON. Sound: C. A. RIGGS. Archery Super-
      visor: HOWARD HILL. Fencing Master: FRED CRAVENS.
      Costumes: MILO ANDERSON. Makeup: PERC WESTMORE.
      Assistant Directors: LEE KATZ and JACK SULLIVAN. Unit
      Production Manager: AL ALLEBORN.
          Cast - ERROL FLYNN (Robin Hood), OLIVIA de HAVILLAND

(Maid Marian), BASIL RATHBONE (Sir Guy of Gisbourne),
CLAUDE RAINS (Prince John), PATRICK KNOWLES (Will
Scarlett), EUGENE PALLETTE (Friar Tuck), ALAN HALE
(Little John), MELVILLE COOPER (High Sheriff of Nottingham),
IAN HUNTER (King Richard the Lion-heart), UNA O'CONNOR
(Bess), HERBERT MUNDIN (Much-the-miller's-son), MONTAGU
LOVE (Bishop of the Black Cannons), LEONARD WILLEY (Sir
Essex), ROBERT NOBLE (Sir Ralf), KENNETH HUNTER (Sir
Mortimer), ROBERT WARWICK (Sir Geoffrey), COLIN KENNY
(Sir Baldwin), LESTER MATTHEWS (Sir Ivor), HARRY
CORDING (Dickon Malbete), HOWARD HILL (Captain of the
Archers), IVAN SIMPSON (Proprietor of the Kent Road tavern),
CHARLES McNAUGHTON (Crippen), LIONEL BELMORE (Humility
Prin), AUSTIN FAIRMAN (Sir Nigel), CRAUFORD KENT (Sir
Norbert), REGINALD SHEFFIELD (Herald at archery tourna-
ment), WILFRED LUCAS (Archery Official), HOLMES HERBERT
(Archery Referee) and JAMES BAKER (Phillip of Arras).

127. Four Daughters - August, 1938. Warner Bros.-First National.
Running time: 90 minutes.
    Credits - Producer: HAL B. WALLIS. Screenplay:
JULIUS J. EPSTEIN and LENORE COFFEE, based on the novel
Sister Act by FANNIE HURST. Camera: ERNEST HALLER,
Art Director: JOHN HUGHES. Editor: RALPH DAWSON.
Music: MAX STEINER.
    Cast - CLAUDE RAINS (Adam Lemp), JEFFREY LYNN
(Felix Deitz), JOHN GARFIELD (Mickey Borden), FRANK
McHUGH (Ben Crowley), MAY ROBSON (Aunt Etta), ROSE-
MARY LANE, LOLA LANE, PRISCILLA LANE and GAIL PAGE
(the Four Daughters) with VERA LEWIS, DICK FORAN, TOM
DUGAN and EDDIE ACUFF.

128. Four's a Crowd - August, 1938. Warner Bros.-First National.
Running time: 91 minutes.
    Credits - Producer: DAVID LEWIS. Screenplay: CASEY
ROBINSON and SIG HERZIG, based on the novel All Rights
Reserved by WALLACE SULLIVAN. Camera: ERNEST HALLER.
Art Director: MAX PARKER. Editor: CLARENCE KOLSTER.
Music: HEINZ ROEMHELD and RAY HEINDORF.
    Cast - ERROL FLYNN (Bob Lansford), OLIVIA de HAVIL-
LAND (Lorri Dillingwell), ROSALIND RUSSELL (Jean Christy),
PATRICK KNOWLES (Patterson Buckley), WALTER CONNOLLY
(John P. Dillingwell) with HUGH HERBERT, MELVILLE
COOPER, FRANKLIN PANGBORN, HERMAN BING, MARGARET
HAMILTON, JOSEPH CREHAN, JOE CUNNINGHAM, DENNIE
MOORE, CAROLE LANDIS, GLORIA BLONDELL and RENÉ
RIVERO.

129. Angels with Dirty Faces - November, 1938. Warner Bros.-
First National. Running time: 97 minutes.
    Credits - Producer: SAMUEL BISCHOFF. Screenplay:

JOHN WEXLEY and WARREN DUFF, from an original story by
ROWLAND BROWN. Camera: SOL POLITO. Art Director:
ROBERT HAAS. Editor: OWEN MARKS. Music: MAX
STEINER. Orchestrations: HUGO FRIEDHOFER. Makeup:
PERC WESTMORE. Dialogue Director: JO GRAHAM.
Assistant Director: SHERRY SHOURDS. Technical Advisor:
FATHER J. J. DEVLIN. Costumes: ORRY-KELLY.

Cast - JAMES CAGNEY (Rocky Sullivan), PAT O'BRIEN
(Father Jerry Connelly), HUMPHREY BOGART (James Frazier),
ANN SHERIDAN (Laury Martin), GEORGE BANCROFT (Mac-
Keefer), BILLY HALOP (Soapy), BOBBY JORDAN (Swing),
LEO GORCEY (Bim), BERNARD PUNSLEY (Hunky), GABRIEL
DELL (Patsy), HUNTZ HALL (Crab), FRANKIE BURKE
(Rocky as a boy), WILLIAM TRACY (Jerry as a boy),
MARILYN KNOWLDEN (Laury as a girl), JOE DOWNING (Steve),
ADRIAN MORRIS (Blackie), OSCAR O'SHEA (Guard Kennedy),
EDWARD PAWLEY (Guard Edwards), WILLIAM PAWLEY (Bugs),
JOHN HAMILTON (Police Captain), EARL DWIRE (Priest),
JACK PERRIN (Death Row Guard), MARY GORDON (Mrs.
Patrick), VERA LEWIS (Soapy's Mother), WILLIAM WORTHING-
TON (Warden), JAMES FARLEY (Railroad Yard Watchman),
CHUCK STUBBS (Red), EDDIE SYRACUSE (Maggione Boy),
ROBERT HOMANS (Policeman), HARRIS BERGER (Basketball
Captain), HARRY HAYDEN (Pharmacist), DICK RICH
(Gangster), STEVEN DARRELL (Gangster), JOE A. DEVLIN
(Gangster), WILLIAM EDMUNDS (Italian Storekeeper),
CHARLES WILSON (Buckley), FRANK COGHLAN, JR. (Boy
in Poolroom), DAVID DURAND (Boy in Poolroom), BILL COHEE,
LAVEL LUND, NORMAN WALLACE, GARY CARTHEW and
BOBBY MAYER (Church Basketball Team), BELLE MITCHELL
(Mrs. Maggione), EDDIE BRIAN (Newsboy), BILLY McLAIN
(Janitor), WILBUR JACK (Croupier), POPPY WILDE (Girl at
Gaming Table), with GEORGE OFFERMAN, JR., CHARLES
TROWBRIDGE, RALPH SANFORD, WILFRED LUCAS, LANE
CHANDLER, ELLIOTT SULLIVAN, LOTTIE WILLIAMS, GEORGE
MORI, DICK WESSELL, JOHN HARRON, VINCE LOMBARDI,
AL HILL, THOMAS JACKSON and JEFFREY SAYRE.

130. Dodge City - April, 1939. Warner Bros.-First National. Running time: 105 minutes.

Credits - Producer: HAL B. WALLIS. Associate Producer:
ROBERT LORD. Screenplay: ROBERT BUCKNER. Camera
(Technicolor): SOL POLITO. Assistant Cameraman: RAY
RENNAHAN. Art Director: TED SMITH. Editor: GEORGE
AMY. Music: MAX STEINER. Orchestrations: HUGO FRIED-
HOFER. Special Effects: BYRON HASKIN and REX WIMPY.
Sound: OLIVER S. GARRETSON. Makeup: PERC WESTMORE.
Costumes: MILO ANDERSON.

Cast - ERROL FLYNN (Wade Hatton), OLIVIA de HAVILLAND
(Abbie Irving), ANN SHERIDAN (Ruby Gilman), BRUCE CABOT
(Jeff Surrett), FRANK McHUGH (Joe Clemens), ALAN HALE

(Rusty Hart), JOHN LITEL (Matt Cole), HENRY TRAVERS
(Doctor Irving), HENRY O'NEILL (Colonel Dodge), VICTOR
JORY (Yancey), WILLIAM LUNDIGAN (Lee Irving), GUINN
"BIG BOY" WILLIAMS (Tex Baird), BOBS WATSON (Harry
Cole), GLORIA HOLDEN (Mrs. Cole), DOUGLAS FOWLEY
(Munger), GEORGIA CAINE (Mrs. Irving), CHARLES HALTON
(Surrett's Lawyer), WARD BOND (Bud Taylor), CORA
WITHERSPOON (Mrs. McCoy), RUSSELL SIMPSON (Orth),
MONTE BLUE (Barlow), NAT CARR (Crocker), CLEM BEVANS
(Barber), JOSEPH CREHAN (Hammond), THURSTON HALL
(Twitchell) and CHESTER CLUTE (Coggins).

131. Sons of Liberty - 1939. Warner Bros.-First National. Running
time: 20 minutes.
    Credits - Producer: GORDON HOLLINGSHEAD. Screen-
play: CRANE WILBUR.
    Cast - CLAUDE RAINS and GALE SONDERGAARD. (This
was Curtiz' only short subject.)

132. Daughters Courageous - June, 1939. Warner Bros.-First
National. Running time: 107 minutes.
    Credits - Producer: HAL B. WALLIS. Associate Producer:
HENRY BLANKE. Screenplay: JULIUS J. EPSTEIN and
PHILIP G. EPSTEIN, adapted from a play by DOROTHY BEN-
NETT based on characters created by FANNIE HURST.
Camera: JAMES WONG HOWE. Editor: RALPH DAWSON.
Music: MAX STEINER.
    Cast - CLAUDE RAINS (Jim Masters), JOHN GARFIELD
(Gabriel Lopez), JEFFREY LYNN (Johnny Henning), FAY
BAINTER (Nan Masters), DONALD CRISP (Sam Sloan) with
FRANK McHUGH, GAIL PAGE, LOLA LANE, PRISCILLA LANE,
ROSEMARY LANE, DICK FORAN, GEORGE HUMBERT and
BERTON CHURCHILL.

133. The Private Lives of Elizabeth and Essex (Reissue title:
Elizabeth the Queen) - December, 1939. Warner Bros.-First
National. Running time: 106 minutes.
    Credits - Producer: HAL B. WALLIS. Associate Producer:
ROBERT LORD. Screenplay: NORMAN REILLY RAINE and
AENEAS MacKENZIE, based on the play Elizabeth the Queen by
MAXWELL ANDERSON. Camera (Technicolor): SOL POLITO.
Technicolor Consultant: MORGAN PADELFORD. Art Director:
ANTON GROT. Music: ERICH WOLFGANG KORNGOLD.
Editor: OWEN MARKS. Special Effects: BYRON HASKIN and
H. F. KOENEKAMP. Makeup: PERC WESTMORE. Costumes:
ORRY-KELLY.
    Cast - BETTE DAVIS (Queen Elizabeth), ERROL FLYNN
(Earl of Essex), OLIVIA de HAVILLAND (Lady Penelope Gray),
DONALD CRISP (Francis Bacon), ALAN HALE (Earl of Tyrone),
VINCENT PRICE (Sir Walter Raleigh), HENRY STEPHENSON
(Lord Burghley), HENRY DANIELL (Sir Robert Cecil), JAMES

STEPHENSON (Sir Thomas Egerton), NANETTE FABRAY
(Mistress Margaret Radcliffe), RALPH FORBES (Lord Knollys),
ROBERT WARWICK (Lord Mountjoy), LEO G. CARROLL (Sir
Edward Coke) with MARIS WRIXON, ROSELLA TOWNE,
FORRESTER HARVEY, JOHN SUTTON, GUY BELLIS, DORIS
LLOYD and I. STANFORD JOLLEY.

134. Four Wives - December, 1939. Warner Bros.-First National.
Running time: 110 minutes.
    Credits - Producer: HAL B. WALLIS. Associate Producer:
HENRY BLANKE. Screenplay: JULIUS J. EPSTEIN and
PHILIP G. EPSTEIN, based on the novel Sister Act by FANNIE
HURST. Camera: SOL POLITO. Art Director: JOHN
HUGHES. Editor: RALPH DAWSON. Music: MAX STEINER.
    Cast - CLAUDE RAINS (Adam Lemp), PRISCILLA LANE
(Ann Lemp Borden), ROSEMARY LANE (Kay Lemp), LOLA
LANE (Thea Lemp Crowley), JEFFREY LYNN (Felix Deitz) with
EDDIE ALBERT, MAY ROBSON, FRANK McHUGH, DICK FORAN,
HENRY O'NEILL, VERA LEWIS and JOHN QUALEN.

135. Virginia City - April, 1940. Warner Bros.-First National.
Running time: 121 minutes.
    Credits - Producer: HAL B. WALLIS. Associate Producer:
ROBERT FELLOWS. Screenplay: ROBERT BUCKNER.
Camera: SOL POLITO. Art Director: TED SMITH. Music:
MAX STEINER. Orchestrations: HUGO FRIEDHOFER. Editor:
GEORGE AMY. Special Effects: BYRON HASKIN and H. F.
KOENEKAMP. Sound: OLIVER S. GARRETSON. and FRANK
J. SCHEID. Makeup: PERC WESTMORE.
    Cast - ERROL FLYNN (Kerry Bradford), MIRIAM HOPKINS
(Julia Hayne), RANDOLPH SCOTT (Vance Irby), HUMPHREY
BOGART (John Murrell), FRANK McHUGH (Mr. Upjohn),
ALAN HALE (Moose), GUINN "BIG BOY" WILLIAMS (Marble-
head), JOHN LITEL (Marshall), DOUGLASS DUMBRILLE (Major
Drewery), MORONI OLSEN (Doctor Cameron), RUSSELL HICKS
(Armistead), DICKIE JONES (Cobby), FRANK WILCOX (Union
Soldier), RUSSELL SIMPSON (Gaylord), VICTOR KILLIAN
(Abraham Lincoln), CHARLES MIDDLETON (Jefferson Davis),
MONTE MONTAGUE (Stage Driver), GEORGE REGAS (Hench-
man), PAUL FIX (Henchman), THURSTON HALL (General
Meade), CHARLES TROWBRIDGE (Seddon), HOWARD HICK-
MAN (General Page), CHARLES HALTON (Ralston), WARD
BOND (Sergeant), SAM McDANIEL (Sam), HARRY CORDING
(Scarecrow), TREVOR BARDETTE (Fanatic), TOM DUGAN
(Spieler), SPENCER CHARTERS (Bartender) and GEORGE
REEVES (Telegrapher).

136. The Sea Hawk - July, 1940. Warner Bros.-First National.
Running time: 127 minutes.
    Credits - Producer: HAL B. WALLIS. Associate Producer:
HENRY BLANKE. Screenplay: HOWARD KOCH and SETON I.

MILLER. Camera: SOL POLITO. Art Director: ANTON
GROT. Music: ERICH WOLFGANG KORNGOLD. Orchestra-
tions: HUGO FRIEDHOFER, MILAN RODER, RAY HEINDORF
and SIMON BUCHAROFF. Musical Director: LEO FORBSTEIN.
Editor: GEORGE AMY. Special Effects: BYRON HASKIN
and H. F. KOENEKAMP. Costumes: ORRY-KELLY. Makeup:
PERC WESTMORE. Sound: FRANCIS J. SCHEID. Fencing
Master: FRED CAVENS. Dialogue Director: JO GRAHAM.
Technical Advisors: ALI HUBERT, THOMAS MANNERS and
WILLIAM KIEL.

Cast - ERROL FLYNN (Geoffrey Thorpe), BRENDA
MARSHALL (Dona Maria), CLAUDE RAINS (Don Jose Alvarez
De Cordoba), DONALD CRISP (Sir John Burleson), FLORA
ROBSON (Queen Elizabeth), ALAN HALE (Carl Pitt), HENRY
DANIELL (Lord Wolfingham), UNA O'CONNOR (Miss Latham),
JAMES STEPHENSON (Abbott), GILBERT ROLAND (Captain
Lopez), WILLIAM LUNDIGAN (Danny Logan), JULIEN MIT-
CHELL (Oliver Scott), MONTAGU LOVE (King Philip II), J.
M. KERRIGAN (Eli Matson), DAVID BRUCE (Martin Burke),
CLIFFORD BROOKE (William Tuttle), FRANK WILCOX (Martin
Barrett), CLYDE COOK (Walter Boggs), HERBERT ANDERSON
(Eph Winters), FRITZ LEIBER (Inquisitor), EDGAR BUCHA-
NAN (Ben Rollins), ELLIS IRVING (Monty Preston), FRANCIS
McDONALD (Kroner), CHARLES ERWIN (Arnold Cross),
PEDRO De CORDOBA (Captain Mendoza), IAN KEITH (Peralta),
JACK LaRUE (Lieutenant Ortega); HALLIWELL HOBBES (As-
tronomer), FRANK LACKTEEN (Captain Ortiz), ALEC CRAIG
(Chartmaker), VICTOR VARCONI (General Aguerra), ROBERT
WARRICK (Martin Frobisher) and GUY BELLIS (John Hawkins).

137. Santa Fe Trail - December, 1940. Warner Bros.-First National.
Running time: 110 minutes.
Credits - Producer: HAL B. WALLIS. Associate Producer:
ROBERT FELLOWS. Screenplay: ROBERT BUCKNER.
Camera: SOL POLITO. Art Director: JOHN HUGHES.
Music: MAX STEINER. Orchestrations: HUGO FRIEDHOFER.
Editor: GEORGE AMY. Special Effects: BYRON HASKIN and
H. F. KOENEKAMP. Sound: ROBERT B. LEE. Costumes:
MILO ANDERSON. Makeup: PERC WESTMORE. Dialogue
Director: JO GRAHAM.

Cast - ERROL FLYNN (Jeb Stuart), OLIVIA de HAVILLAND
(Kit Carson Halliday), RAYMOND MASSEY (John Brown),
RONALD REAGAN (George Armstrong Custer), ALAN HALE
(Tex Bell), WILLIAM LUNDIGAN (Bob Halliday), VAN HEFLIN
(Rader), GENE REYNOLDS (Jason Brown), HENRY O'NEILL
(Cyrus Halliday), GUINN "BIG BOY" WILLIAMS (Windy Brody),
ALAN BAXTER (Oliver Brown), JOHN LITEL (Martin),
MORONI OLSEN (Robert E. Lee), DAVID BRUCE (Phil Sheri-
dan), HOBART CAVANAUGH (Barber Doyle), CHARLES D.
BROWN (Major Sumner), JOSEPH SAWYER (Kitzmiller), FRANK
WILCOX (James Longstreet), WARD BOND (Townley), RUSSELL

SIMPSON (Shoubel Morgan), CHARLES MIDDLETON (Gentry),
ERVILLE ALDERSON (Jefferson Davis), SPENCER CHARTERS
(Conductor), SUZANNE CARNAHAN (Charlotte), WILLIAM
MARSHALL (George Pickett), GEORGE HAYWOOD (John Hood),
WILFRED LUCAS (Weiner) and RUSSELL HICKS (J. Boyce
Russell).

138. The Sea Wolf - March, 1941. Warner Bros.-First National.
Running time: 90 minutes.
    Credits - Producer: HAL B. WALLIS. Associate Producer:
HENRY BLANKE. Screenplay: ROBERT ROSSEN, adapted
from the novel by JACK LONDON. Camera: SOL POLITO.
Art Director: ANTON GROT. Editor: GEORGE AMY. Music:
ERICH WOLFGANG KORNGOLD. Sound: OLIVER S. GARRET-
SON. Special Effects: BYRON HASKIN and H. F. KOENE-
KAMP.
    Cast - EDWARD G. ROBINSON (Wolf Larsen), IDA LUPINO
(Ruth Webster), JOHN GARFIELD (George Leach), GENE
LOCKHART (Louie), BARRY FITZGERALD (Cooky), with
ALEXANDER KNOX, STANLEY RIDGES, DAVID BRUCE, FRAN-
CIS McDONALD, HOWARD Da SILVA, FRANK LACKTEEN and
WILFRED LUCAS.

139. Dive Bomber - August, 1941. Warner Bros.-First National.
Running time: 133 minutes.
    Credits - Producer: HAL B. WALLIS. Associate Producer:
ROBERT LORD. Screenplay: FRANK WEAD and ROBERT
BUCKNER, based on an original story by FRANK WEAD.
Camera (Technicolor): BERT GLENNON and WINTON C. HOCH.
Aerial Photography: ELMER DYER and CHARLES MARSHALL.
Technicolor Color Consultant: NATALIE KALMUS. Art
Director: ROBERT HAAS. Editor: GEORGE AMY. Music:
MAX STEINER. Orchestrations: HUGO FRIEDHOFER.
Special Effects: BYRON HASKIN and REX WIMPY. Sound:
FRANCIS J. SCHEID. Makeup: PERC WESTMORE. Chief
Pilot: PAUL MANTZ. Aeronautical Technical Advisor: S. H.
WARNER, commander, USN. Medical Technical Advisor:
J. R. POPPEN, Captain (MC), USN. Assistant Director:
SHERRY SHOURDS.
    Cast - ERROL FLYNN (Lieutenant Douglas Lee), FRED
MacMURRAY (Commander Joe Blake), RALPH BELLAMY (Dr.
Lance Rogers), ALEXIS SMITH (Linda Fisher), ROBERT
ARMSTRONG (Art Lyons), REGIS TOOMEY (Tim Griffin),
ALLEN JENKINS (Lucky James), CRAIG STEVENS (John
Thomas Anthony), HERBERT ANDERSON (Chubby), MORONI
OLSEN (Senior Flight Surgeon), DENNIE MOORE (Mrs. James),
LOUIS JEAN HEYDT (Swede Larson), CLIFF NAZARRO (Corps
Man), ANN DORAN (Helen), ADDISON RICHARDS (Senior
FLIGHT SURGEON), RUSSELL HICKS (Admiral), HOWARD
HICKMAN (Admiral) with WILLIAM HOPPER, CHARLES DRAKE,
BYRON BARR, LARRY WILLIAMS, GARLAND SMITH, TOM

SKINNER, TOM SEIDEL, GAYLORD PENDLETON, LYLE
MORAINE, GARRETT CRAIG, JAMES ANDERSON, STANLEY
SMITH, DAVID NEWELL, ALAN HALE, JR., SOL GROSS and
DON TURNER.

140. Captains of the Clouds - January, 1942. Warner Bros.-First
National. Running time: 113 minutes.
    Credits - Producer: HAL B. WALLIS. Associate Producer:
WILLIAM CAGNEY. Screenplay: ARTHUR T. HORMAN,
RICHARD MacAULAY and NORMAN REILLY RAINE, based on
a story by ARTHUR T. HORMAN AND ROLAND GILLETT.
Camera (Technicolor): SOL POLITO and WILFRED M. CLINE.
Aerial Photography: ELMER DYER, CHARLES MARSHALL and
WINTON C. HOCH. Technical Color Consultant: NATALIE
KALMUS. Art Director: TED SMITH. Editor: GEORGE AMY.
Music: MAX STEINER. Musical Director: LEO FORBSTEIN.
Special Effects: BYRON HASKIN and REX WIMPY. Sound:
C. A. RIGGS. Costumes: HOWARD SHOUP. Chief Pilot:
FRANK CLARKE. Technical Advisor: O. CATHCART JONES.
    Cast - JAMES CAGNEY (Brian MacLean), DENNIS MORGAN
(Johnny Dutton), BRENDA MARSHALL (Emily Foster), ALAN
HALE (Tiny Murphy), GEORGE TOBIAS (Blimp Lebec),
REGINALD GARDINER (Scrounger Harris), Air Marshal W. A.
BISHOP (himself), REGINALD DENNY (Commanding Officer),
RUSSELL ARMS (Prentiss), PAUL CAVANAUGH (Group Cap-
tain), CLEM BEVANS (Store-teeth Morrison), J. M. KERRI-
GAN (Foster), J. FARRELL MacDONALD (Doctor Neville),
PATRICK O'MCORE (Fyffo), MORTON LOWRY (Carmichael),
O. CATHCART JONES (Chief Instructor), FREDERIC WORLOCK
(President of Court Martial), ROLAND DREW (Officer), LUCIA
CARROLL (Blonde) with GEORGE MEEKER, BENNY BAKER,
HARDIE ALBRIGHT, ROY WALKER, CHARLES HALTON, LOUIS
JEAN HEYDT, BYRON BARR, MICHAEL AMES, WILLIE FUNG,
CARL HARBORD, JAMES STEVENS, BILL WILKERSON, FRANK
LACKTEEN, EDWARD McNAMARA, CHARLES SMITH, EMMETT
VOGAN, WINIFRED HARRIS, MILES MANDER, PAT FLAHERTY,
TOM DUGAN, GEORGE OFFERMAN, JR., GAVIN MUIR, LARRY
WILLIAMS, JOHN HARTLEY, JOHN KELLOGG, CHARLES IRWIN,
BILLY WAYNE, RAFAEL STORM, JOHN GALLAUDET, BARRY
BERNARD, GEORGE OVEY, WALTER BROOKS, RAY MONT-
GOMERY, HERBERT GUNN, DONALD DILLAWAY and JAMES
BUSH.

141. Yankee Doodle Dandy - May, 1942. Warner Bros.-First
National. Running time: 126 minutes.
    Credits - Producer: HAL B. WALLIS. Associate Producer:
WILLIAM CAGNEY. Screenplay: ROBERT BUCKNER and
EDMUND JOSEPH, based on a story by ROBERT BUCKNER.
Camera: JAMES WONG HOWE. Art Director: CARL JULES
WEYL. Editor: GEORGE AMY. Montages: DON SIEGEL.
Musical Adaptations: HEINZ ROEMHELD. Orchestrations:

RAY HEINDORF. Musical Director: LEO FORBSTEIN.
Songs--"I Was Born in Virginia," "The Warmest Baby in the
Bunch," "Give My Regards to Broadway," "Mary's a Grand
Old Name," "So Long Mary," "Yankee Doodle Boy," "Over
There," "Harrigan," "Forty-five Minutes from Broadway," and
"You're a Grand Old Flag": GEORGE M. COHAN. New Song
--"All Aboard for Old Broadway": JACK SCHOLL and
M. K. JEROME. Choreography: LEROY PRINZ, SEYMOUR
FELIX and JOHN BOYLE. Sound: EVERETT A. BROWN.
Costumes: MILO ANDERSON. Dialogue Director: HUGH
MacMULLAN.
     Cast - JAMES CAGNEY (George M. Cohan), JOAN LESLIE
(Mary), WALTER HUSTON (Jerry Cohan), RICHARD WHORF
(Sam Harris), GEORGE TOBIAS (Dietz), IRENE MANNING
(Fay Templeton), ROSEMARY De CAMP (Nellie Cohan),
JEANNE CAGNEY (Josie Cohan), S. Z. SAKALL (Schwab),
GEORGE BARBIER (Erlanger), WALTER CATLETT (Manager),
FRANCES LANGFORD (Nora Bayes), MINOR WATSON (Ed
Albee), EDDIE FOY, JR. (Eddie Foy), CHESTER CLUTE
(Harold Goff), DOUGLAS CROFT (George M. Cohan at age 13),
PATSY LEE PARSONS (Josie at age 12), Captain JACK YOUNG
(Franklin D. Roosevelt), AUDREY LONG (Receptionist),
ODETTE MYRTIL (Madame Bartholdi), CLINTON ROSEMOND
(White House Butler), SPENCER CHARTERS (Stage Manager),
DOROTHY KELLY and MARI JO JAMES (Sister Act), HENRY
BLAIR (George M. Cohan at age 7), JO ANN MARLOW (Josie
Cohan at age 6), THOMAS JACKSON (Stage Manager),
PHYLLIS KENNEDY (Fanny), PAT FLAHERTY (White House
Guard), LEON BELASCO (Magician), SYD SAYLOR (Star
Boarder), WILLIAM B. DAVIDSON (Stage Manager), HARRY
HAYDEN (Doctor Lewellyn), FRANCIS PIERLOT (Doctor
Anderson), CHARLES SMITH, JOYCE REYNOLDS, DICK
CHANDLEE and JOYCE HORNE (Teenagers), FRANK FAYLEN
(Sergeant), WALLIS CLARK (Theodore Roosevelt), GEORGIA
CARROLL (Betsy Ross), JOAN WINFIELD (Sally), DICK
WESSEL and JAMES FLAVIN (Union Army Veterans), SAILOR
VINCENT (Schultz in Peck's Bad Boy), FRED KELSEY (Irish
Cop in Peck's Bad Boy), GEORGE MEEKER and FRANK MAYO
(Hotel Clerks), TOM DUGAN (Actor), CREIGHTON HALE
(Telegraph Operator), MURRAY ALPER (Wise Guy), GARY
OWEN (Army Clerk), RUTH ROBINSON (Nurse), EDDIE ACUFF,
WALTER BROOKE, BILL EDWARDS and WILLIAM HOPPER
(Reporters), WILLIAM FORREST (1st Critic), ED KEANE (2nd
Critic), DOLORES MORAN (Girl), POPPY WILDE (Chorus Girl),
and LORRAINE GETTMAN (Chorus Girl).

142. Mission to Moscow - April, 1943. Warner Bros.-First National.
      Running time: 123 minutes.
           Credits - Producer: ROBERT BUCKNER. Screenplay:
      HOWARD KOCH, based on the book by JOSEPH DAVIES.
      Camera: BERT GLENNON. Art Director: CARL JULES WEYL.

Editor: OWEN MARKS. Montages: DON SIEGEL and JAMES
LEICESTER. Music: MAX STEINER. Technical Advisor:
JAY LEYDA.

Cast - WALTER HUSTON (Joseph E. Davies), ANN HARDING
(Mrs. Davies), OSCAR HOLMOLKA (Maxim Litvinov), GEORGE
TOBIAS (Freddie), GENE LOCKHART (Molotov) with HENRY
DANIELL, FRIEDA INESCOURT, ELEANOR PARKER, RICHARD
TRAVIS, HELMUT DANTINE, VICTOR FRANCEN, BARBARA
EVEREST, DUDLEY FIELD MALONE, ROMAN BOHNEN, MARIA
PALMER, MORONI OLSEN, MINOR WATSON, JEROME COWAN,
FRANK PUGLIA, DUNCAN RENALDO, GLENN STRANGE, FRANK
FAYLEN, PIERRE WATKIN, EDWARD VON SLOAN, MICHAEL
MARK and CYD CHARISSE.

143. This Is the Army - July, 1943. Warner Bros.-First National.
Running time: 121 minutes.

Credits - Producer: HAL B. WALLIS. Screenplay: CASEY
ROBINSON and Captain CLAUDE BINYON, from a story by
IRVING BERLIN. Camera (Technicolor): BERT GLENNON and
SOL POLITO. Art Director: JOHN HUGHES. Editor: GEORGE
AMY. Music: IRVING BERLIN.

Cast - GEORGE MURPHY (Jerry Jones), JOAN LESLIE
(Eileen Dibble), GEORGE TOBIAS (Maxie Twardofsky), ALAN
HALE (Sergeant McGhee), CHARLES BUTTERWORTH (Eddie
Dibble) with RONALD REAGAN, JOE LOUIS, DOLORES
COSTELLO, UNA MERKEL, STANLEY RIDGES, ROSEMARY De
CAMP, KATE SMITH, RUTH DONNELLY, DOROTHY PETERSON,
FRANCES LANGFORD, GERTRUDE NIESEN and ILKA GRUNING.

144. Casablanca - November, 1943. Warner Bros.-First National.
Running time: 102 minutes.

Credits - Producer: HAL B. WALLIS. Screenplay:
JULIUS J. EPSTEIN, PHILIP G. EPSTEIN and HOWARD KOCH,
based on the play Everybody Comes to Rick's by MURRAY
BURNETT and JOAN ALISON. Camera: ARTHUR EDESON.
Art Director: CARL JULES WEYL. Set Decorator: GEORGE
JAMES HOPKINS. Editor: OWEN MARKS. Montages: DON
SIEGEL and JAMES LEICESTER. Music: MAX STEINER.
Orchestrations: HUGO FRIEDHOFER. Songs--"As Time Goes
By": HERMAN HUPFELD, "Knock on Wood": M. K. JEROME
and JACK SCHOLL. Special Effects: LAWRENCE BUTLER
and WILLARD VAN ENGER. Sound: FRANCIS J. SCHEID.
Narrator: LOU MARCELLE. Gowns: ORRY-KELLY. Techni-
cal Advisor: ROBERT AISNER. Assistant Director: LEE
KATZ.

Cast - HUMPHREY BOGART (Rick Blaine), INGRID BERG-
MAN (Ilsa), PAUL HENREID (Victor Laszlo), CLAUDE RAINS
(Captain Louis Renault), CONRAD VEIDT (Major Strasser),
SYDNEY GREENSTREET (Senor Farrari), PETER LORRE
(Ugarte), S. Z. SAKALL (Carl), MADELEINE LeBEAU (Yvonne),
DOOLEY WILSON (Sam), JOY PAGE (Annina Brandel), JOHN

QUALEN (Berger), LEONID KINSKY (Sascha), HELMUT
DANTINE (Jan Brandel), CURT BOIS (Pickpocket), MARCEL
DALIO (Croupier), CORINNA MURA (Singer), LUDWIG
STOSSEL (Mr. Leuchtag), ILKA GRUNING (Mrs. Leuchtag),
CHARLES La TORRE (Italian Officer Tonelli), FRANK PUGLIA
(Arab Vendor), DAN SEYMOUR (Abdul).

145. Passage to Marseille - February, 1944. Warner Bros.-First
National. Running time: 110 minutes.
     Credits - Producer: HAL B. WALLIS. Screenplay:
CASEY ROBINSON and JACK MOFFITT, based on the novel
Men Without Country by CHARLES NORDHOFF and JAMES
NORMAN HALL. Camera: JAMES WONG HOWE. Art Director:
CARL JULES WEYL. Set Decotrator: GEORGE JAMES
HOPKINS. Editor: OWEN MARKS. Montages: JAMES
LEICESTER. Music: MAX STEINER. Orchestrations: LEONID
RAAB. Song--"Someday I'll Meet You Again": MAX STEINER
and NED WASHINGTON. Special Effects: JACK COSGROVE,
EDWIN B. DuPAR, BYRON HASKIN and E. ROY DAVIDSON.
Makeup: PERC WESTMORE. Gowns: LEAH RHODES.
     Cast - HUMPHREY BOGART (Matrac), CLAUDE RAINS
(Captain Freycinet), MICHELE MORGAN (Paula), PHILIP DORN
(Renault), SYDNEY GREENSTREET (Major Duval), PETER
LORRE (Marius), GEORGE TOBIAS (Petit), HELMUT DANTINE
(Garou), JOHN LODER (Manning), VICTOR FRANCEN (Captain
Malo) with VLADIMIR SOKOLOFF, EDUARDO CIANELLI,
CORINNA MURA, KONSTANTIN SHAYNE, STEPHEN RICHARDS,
CHARLES La TORRE, HANS CONRIED and MONTE BLUE.

146. Janie - July, 1944. Warner Bros.-First National. Running
time: 106 minutes.
     Credits - Producer: ALEX GOTTLIEB. Screenplay:
CHARLES HOFFMAN and AGNES CHRISTINE JOHNSTON, based
on a play by JOSEPHINE BUTLER and HERSCHEL W.
WILLIAMS, JR. Camera: CARL GUTHRIE. Art Director:
ROBERT HAAS. Editor: OWEN MARKS. Music: HEINZ
ROEMHELD.
     Cast - JOYCE REYNOLDS (Janie), ROBERT HUTTON (Dick
Lawrence), EDWARD ARNOLD (Charles Conway), ANN
HARDING (Lucille Conway), ROBERT BENCHLEY (John Van
Brunt), with RUTH TOBEY, VIRGINIA PATTON, COLLEEN
TOWNSEND, GEORGIA LEE SETTLE, WILLIAM FRAMBES,
PETER STACKPOLE, RUSSELL HICKS, MICHAEL HARRISON,
ALAN HALE, CLARA FOLEY, BARBARA BROWN, HATTIE
McDANIEL, DICK ERDMAN and ANN GILLIS.

147. Mildred Pierce - September, 1945. Warner Bros.-First National.
Running time: 109 minutes.
     Credits - Producer: JERRY WALD. Screenplay: RANALD
MacDOUGALL and CATHERINE TURNEY, based on the novel by
JAMES M. CAIN. Camera: ERNEST HALLER. Art Director:

ANTON GROT. Editor: DAVID WEISBART. Music: MAX STEINER.

Cast - JOAN CRAWFORD (Mildred Pierce), JACK CARSON (Wally), ZACHARY SCOTT (Monty Berrigan), ANN BLYTH (Veda Pierce), BRUCE BENNETT (Pierce) with EVE ARDEN, JO ANN MARLOWE, MARGARET KIPPEN, LEE PATRICK, MORONI OLSEN, BUTTERFLY McQUEEN, GEORGE TOBIAS, JOHN SHEFFIELD, BARBARA BROWN, CHESTER CLUTE, JOHN COMPTON and CHARLES TROWBRIDGE.

148. Roughly Speaking - October, 1945. Warner Bros.-First National. Running time: 117 minutes.

Credits - Producer: HENRY BLANKE. Screenplay: LOUISE RANDALL PIERSON. Camera: JOSEPH WALKER. Art Director: ROBERT HAAS. Editor: DAVID WEISBART. Music: MAX STEINER.

Cast - ROSALIND RUSSELL (Louise Randall), JACK CARSON (Harold Pierson), ALAN HALE (Mr. Morton), DONALD WOODS (Rodney Crane), ROBERT HUTTON (John) with JEAN SULLIVAN, ANDREA KING, RAY COLLINS, ANN E. TODD, ANDY CLYDE, ARTHUR SHIELDS, ANN DORAN, HOBART CAVANAUGH, JOHN ALVIN, CRAIG STEVENS, FRANCIS PIERLOT, MANART KIPPEN, GEORGE CARLETON, GEORGE MENDER, FRANK PUGLIA, JOHN QUALEN, CHESTER CLUTE, IRVING BACON, BARBARA BROWN, SIG ARNO, ANN LAWRENCE, MONA FREEMAN, MICKEY KUHN, JOHNNY TREAL, JOHN COLKINS, JO ANN MARLOWE, JOHNNY SHEFFIELD, ROBERT ARTHUR and GEORGE MORADIAN.

149. Night and Day - July, 1946. Warner Bros.-First National. Running time: 128 minutes.

Credits - Producer: ARTHUR SCHWARTZ. Screenplay: CHARLES HOFFMAN, LEO TOWNSEND and WILLIAM BOWERS, adaptation by JACK MOFFITT. Camera (Technicolor): J. PEVERELL MARLEY and WILLIAM V. SKALL. Art Director: JOHN HUGHES. Editor: DAVID WEISBART. Music: COLE PORTER and MAX STEINER. Special Effects: ROBERT BURKS.

Cast - CARY GRANT (Cole Porter), ALEXIS SMITH (Linda Lee), MONTY WOOLLEY (himself), GINNY SIMMS (Carole Hill), JANE WYMAN (Gracie Harris), with VICTOR FRANCEN, EVE ARDEN, MARY MARTIN, ALAN HALE, DOROTHY MALONE, TOM D'ANDREA, SELENA ROYLE, DONALD WOODS, SIG RUMAN, HENRY STEPHENSON, PAUL CAVANAUGH, CARLOS RAMIREZ, MILADA MLADOVA, GEORGE ZORITCH, CLARENCE MUSE, JOHN PEARSON, GEORGE RILEY, JOHN ALVIN, HERMAN BING and BILLY WATSON.

150. Life with Father - August, 1947. Warner Bros.-First Naitonal. Running time: 118 minutes.

Credits - Producer: ROBERT BUCKNER. Screenplay: DONALD OGDEN STEWART. Camera (Technicolor):

J. PEVERELL MARLEY and WILLIAM V. SKALL. Art Director:
ROBERT HAAS. Editor: GEORGE AMY. Music: MAX
STEINER.

Cast - WILLIAM POWELL (Father), IRENE DUNNE (Vinnie),
ELIZABETH TAYLOR (Mary), EDMUND GWENN (Reverend
Doctor Lloyd), ZASU PITTS (Cora) with JIMMY LYDON,
EMMA DUNN, MORONI OLSEN, ELIZABETH RISDON, DEREK
SCOTT, JOHN CALKINS, MONTE BLUE, MARTIN MILNER,
HEATHER WILDE, MARY FIELD, NANCY EVANS, QUEENIE
LEONARD, CLARA BLANDICK, FRANK ELLIOTT and DOUGLAS
KENNEDY.

151.   The Unsuspected - October, 1947. Warner Bros.-First
National. Running time: 103 minutes.
Credits - Producer: CHARLES HOFFMAN. Screenplay:
RANALD MacDOUGALL, from a story by CHARLOTTE ARM-
STRONG, adaptation by BEN MEREDYTH. Camera: WOODY
BREDELL. Art Director: ANTON GROT. Editor: FREDERICK
RICHARDS. Music: FRANZ WAXMAN.
Cast - CLAUDE RAINS (Victor Grandison), JOAN CAUL-
FIELD (Matilda Frazier), AUDREY TOTTER (Althea Keane),
CONSTANCE BENNETT (Jane Moynihan), HURD HATFIELD
(Oliver Keane) with MICHAEL NORTH, FRED CLARK, JACK
LAMBERT, HARRY LEWIS, RAY WALKER, WALTER BALDWIN,
NANA BRYANT, GEORGE ELDREDGE, DOUGLAS KENNEDY and
RORY MALLINSON.

152.   Romance on the High Seas - June, 1948. Warner Bros.-First
National. Running time: 99 minutes.
Credits - Producer: ALEX GOTTLIEB. Screenplay:
JULIUS J. EPSTEIN and PHILIP G. EPSTEIN, from a story by
S. PONDAL RIOS and CARLOS A. OLIVARI. Camera
(Technicolor): WOODY BREDELL. Art Director: ANTON
GROT. Editor: RUDI FEHR. Musical Director: LEO
FORBSTEIN.
Cast - DORIS DAY (Georgia Garrett), JACK CARSON
(Peter Virgil), JANIS PAIGE (Elvira Kent), DON DeFORE
(Michael Kent), OSCAR LEVANT (Oscar Farrar) with S. Z.
SAKALL, ERIC BLORE, FRANKLIN PANGBORN, FORTUNIO
BONANOVA, LESLIE BROOKS, WILLIAM BAKEWELL, JOHNNY
BERKES, AVON LONG, KENNETH BRITTON, SIR LANCELOT,
THE SAMBA KINGS and THE PAGE CAVANAUGH TRIO.

153.   My Dream Is Yours - March, 1949. Warner Bros.-First
National. Running time: 101 minutes.
Credits - Producer: MICHAEL CURTIZ. Screenplay:
HARRY KURNITZ and DANE LURRIER. Camera (Technicolor):
ERNEST HALLER. Art Director: ROBERT HAAS. Editor:
FORMAR BLANGSTEAD. Music: HARRY WARREN.
Cast - DORIS DAY (Martha Gibson), JACK CARSON (Doug
Blake), LEE BOWMAN (Gary Mitchell), ADOLPHE MENJOU

(Thomas Hutchings), EVE ARDEN (Vivian Martin) with
S. Z. SAKALL, SELENA ROYLE, EDGAR KENNEDY, SHELDON
LEONARD, FRANKIE CARLE, DUNCAN RICHARDSON, JOHN
BERKES and ADA LEONARD.

154. Flamingo Road - May, 1949. Warner Bros.-First National.
Running time: 94 minutes.
      Credits - Producer: JERRY WALD. Screenplay: ROBERT
WILDER, from the play by ROBERT WILDER and SALLY
WILDER. Camera: TED McCORD. Art Director: LEO K.
KUTER. Editor: FOLMAR BLANGSTEAD. Music: RAY
HEINDORF.
      Cast - JOAN CRAWFORD (Lane Bellamy), ZACHARY SCOTT
(Fielding Carlisle), SYDNEY GREENSTREET (Titus Semple),
DAVID BRIAN (Dan Reynolds), GLADYS GEORGE (Lute Mae
Saunders) with VIRGINIA HUSTON, FRED CLARK, ALICE
WHITE, GERTRUDE MICHAEL, SAM McDANIEL and TITO
VUOLO.

155. The Lady Takes a Sailor - November, 1949. Warner Bros.-
First National. Running time: 99 minutes.
      Credits - Producer: HARRY KURNITZ. Screenplay:
EVERETT FREEMAN, from a story by JERRY GRASKIN.
Camera: TED McCORD. Editor: DAVID WEISBART. Music:
MAX STEINER.
      Cast - JANE WYMAN (Jennifer), DENNIS MORGAN (Bill),
EVE ARDEN (Susan), ROBERT DOUGLAS (Tyson), ALLYN
JOSLYN (Ralph Whitcomb) with TOM TULLY, LINA RONAY,
FRED CLARK, WILLIAM FRAWLEY, CHARLES MEREDITH,
CRAIG STEVENS, STANLEY PRAGER and KENNETH BRITTON.

156. Young Man with a Horn - February, 1950. Warner Bros.-
First National. Running time: 112 minutes.
      Credits - Producer: JERRY WALD. Screenplay: CARL
FOREMAN and EDMUND H. NORTH, based on a novel by
DOROTHY BAKER. Camera: TED McCORD. Art Director:
EDWARD CARRERE. Editor: ALAN CROSLAND, JR. Music:
RAY HEINDORF. Trumpet Music: HARRY JAMES.
      Cast - KIRK DOUGLAS (Rick Martin), LAUREN BACALL
(Amy North), DORIS DAY (Jo Jordan), HOAGY CARMICHAEL
(Smoke Willoughby), JUANO HERNANDEZ (Art Hazard) with
JEROME COWAN, MARY BETH HUGHES, ORLEY LINDGREN,
NESTOR PAIVA and DAN SEYMOUR.

157. Bright Leaf - June, 1950. Warner Bros.-First National.
Running time: 110 minutes.
      Credits - Producer: HENRY BLANKE. Screenplay:
RANALD MacDOUGALL, based on a story by FOSTER
FITZSIMMONS. Camera: KARL FREUND. Art Director:
STANLEY FLEISCHER. Editor: OWEN MARKS. Music:
VICTOR YOUNG.

Cast - GARY COOPER (Brant Royle), LAUREN BACALL
(Sonja Kovac), PATRICIA NEAL (Margaret Jane Singleton),
JACK CARSON (Chris Malley), DONALD CRISP (Major James
Singleton) with JEFF COREY, GLADYS GEORGE, ELIZABETH
PATTERSON, TAYLOR HOLMES, THURSTON HALL, JIMMY
GRIFFITH, MARIETTA CANTY and WILLIAM WALKER.

158. The Breaking Point - October, 1950. Warner Bros.-First
National. Running time: 97 minutes.
     Credits - Producer: JERRY WALD. Screenplay: RANALD
MacDOUGALL, based on the novel To Have and Have Not by
ERNEST HEMINGWAY. Camera: TED McCORD. Art Director:
EDWARD CARRERE. Editor: ALAN CROSLAND, JR. Music:
RAY HEINDORF.
     Cast - JOHN GARFIELD (Harry Morgan), PATRICIA NEAL
(Leona Charles), PHYLLIS THAXTER (Lucy Morgan), JUANO
HERNANDEZ (Wesley Park), WALLACE FORD (Duncan) with
EDMOND RYAN, RALPH DUMKE, GUY THOMAJAN, PETER
BROCCO, WILLIAM CAMPBELL, JOHN DOUCETTE, JAMES
GRIFFITH, VICTOR SEN YOUNG, DONNA JO BOYCE and
SHERRY JACKSON.

159. Jim Thorpe-All American - June, 1951. Warner Bros.-First
National. Running time: 107 minutes.
     Credits - Producer: EVERETT FREEMAN. Screenplay:
DOUGLAS MORROW and EVERETT FREEMAN. Camera:
ERNEST HALLER. Art Director: EDWARD CARRERE. Editor:
FOLMAR BLANGSTED. Music: MAX STEINER.
     Cast - BURT LANCASTER (Jim Thorpe), CHARLES BICK-
FORD (Pop Warner), STEVE COCHRAN (Peter Allendine),
PHYLLIS THAXTER (Margaret Miller), DICK WESSON (Ed
Guyac) with JACK BIG HEAD, SUNI WARCLOUD, AL MEJIA,
HUBIE KERNS, BILLY GRAY, NESTOR PAIVA and JIMMY
MOSS.

160. Force of Arms (Reissue title: A Girl for Joe) - August, 1951.
Warner Bros.-First National. Running time: 100 minutes.
     Credits - Producer: ANTHONY VEILLER. Screenplay:
ORIN JANNINGS, based on a story by RICHARD TREGASKIN.
Camera: TED McCORD. Art Director: EDWARD CARRERE.
Editor: OWEN MARKS. Music: MAX STEINER.
     Cast - WILLIAM HOLDEN (Peterson), NANCY OLSON
(Eleanor), FRANK LOVEJOY (Major Blackford), GENE EVANS
(McFee), DICK WESSON (Klein) with PAUL PICERNI, ROSS
FORD, KATHERINE WARREN, RON HAGERTHY, ARGENTINA
BRUNETTI, MARIO SILETTI, AMELIA COVA, DON GORDON,
BOB ROARK and SLATTS TAYLOR.

161. The Story of Will Rogers - June, 1952. Warner Bros.-First
National. Running time: 109 minutes.
     Credits - Producer: ROBERT ARTHUR. Screenplay:

STANLEY ROBERTS and FRANK DAVIS. Camera (Warnercolor): WILFRED M. CLINE. Art Director: EDWARD CARRERE. Editor: FOLMAR BLANGSTED. Music: VICTOR YOUNG.

Cast - WILL ROGERS, JR. (Will Rogers), JANE WYMAN (Mrs. Rogers), JAMES GLEASON (Bert Lynn), CARL BENTON REID (Clem Rogers), EDDIE CANTOR (himself) with EVE MILLER, NOAH BEERY, JR., RICHARD KEAN, SLIM PICKENS, MARY WICKES, STEVE BRODIE, VIRGIL S. TAYLOR, PINKY TOMLIN, MARGARET FIELD, BRYAN DALY, JAY SILVER-HEELS, WILLIAM FORREST and EARL LEE.

162. I'll See You in My Dreams - December, 1952. Warner Bros.-First National. Running time: 110 minutes.

Credits - Producer: LOUIS F. EDELMAN. Screenplay: JACK ROSE and MELVILLE SHAVELSON. Camera (Warnercolor): TED McCORD. Art Director: DOUGLAS BACON. Editor: OWEN MARKS. Music: GUS KAHN. Orchestrations: RAY HEINDORF.

Cast - DANNY THOMAS (Gus Kahn), DORIS DAY (Grace LeBoy Kahn), FRANK LOVEJOY (Walter Donaldson), PATRICIA WYMORE (Gloria Knight), JAMES GLEASON (Fred Thompson) with MARY WICKES, JIM BACKUS, JULIE OSHINS, MINNA GOMBEL, WILLIAM FORREST, HARRY ANTRIM, ELSIE NEFT, DICK SIMMONS, ROBERT LYDEN, BUNNY LEWBEL, MIMI GIBSON and CHRISTY OLSON.

163. The Jazz Singer - January, 1953. Warner Bros.-First National. Running time: 107 minutes.

Credits - Producer: LOUIS F. EDELMAN. Screenplay: FRANK DAVIS, LEONARD STERN and LOUIS MELTZER, based on the play by SAMSON RAPHAELSON. Camera (Warnercolor): CARL GUTHRIE. Art Director: LEO K. KUTER. Editor: ALAN CROSLAND, JR. Music: RAY HEINDORF.

Cast - DANNY THOMAS (Jerry Golding), PEGGY LEE (Judy Lane), MILDRED DUNNOCK (Mrs. Golding), EDUARD FRANZ (Cantor Golding), TOM TULLY (McGURNEY) with ALEX GERAY, HAROLD GORDON and ALLYN JOSLYN.

164. Trouble Along the Way - May, 1953. Warner Bros.-First National. Running time: 110 minutes.

Credits - Producer: MELVILLE SHAVELSON. Screenplay: MELVILLE SHAVELSON and JACK ROSE, based on a story by DOUGLAS MORROW and ROBERT HARDY. Camera: ARCHIE STOUT. Art Director: LEO K. KUTER. Editor: OWEN MARKS. Music: MAX STEINER.

Cast - JOHN WAYNE (Steve Williams), DONNA REED (Alice Singleton), CHARLES COBURN (Father Burke), TOM TULLY (Father Malone), SHERRY JACKSON (Carol) with MARIE WINDSOR, DABBS GREER, TOM HELMORE, LEIF ERICSON, DOUGLAS SPENCER, LESTER MATTHEWS, CHUCK CONNORS and BILL RADOVICH.

165. The Boy from Oklahoma - February, 1954. Warner Bros.-
First National. Running time: 88 minutes.
     Credits - Producer: DAVID WEISBART. Screenplay:
WINSTON MILLER and FRANK DAVIS, from a story by MICHAEL
FERRIER. Camera (Warnercolor): ROBERT BURKES. Art
Director: LEO K. KUTER. Editor: JAMES MOORE. Music:
MAX STEINER.
     Cast - WILL ROGERS, JR. (Tom Brewster), NANCY OLSON
(Katie Brannigan), LON CHANEY, JR. (Crazy Charlie),
ANTHONY CARUSO (Barney Turlock), WALLACE FORD (Wally
Higgins) with LOUIS JEAN HEYDT, CLEM BEVANS, MERV
GRIFFIN, SLIM PICKENS, TYLER MacDUFF, SHEB WOOLEY,
JAMES GRIFFITH, SKIPPY TORGENSON and CHARLES WATTS.

166. The Egyptian - August, 1954. Twentieth Century-Fox.
Running time: 140 minutes.
     Credits - Producer: DARRYL F. ZANUCK. Screenplay:
PHILIP DUNNE and CASEY ROBINSON, based on the novel by
MIKA WALTARI. Camera (De Luxe Color and Cinemascope):
LEON SHAMROY. Art Directors: LYLE R. WHEELER and
GEORGE W. DAVIS. Editor: BARBARA McLEAN. Music:
ALFRED NEWMAN and BERNARD HERRMANN.
     Cast - JEAN SIMMONS (Merit), VICTOR MATURE (Horenheb),
GENE TIERNEY (Baketamon), MICHAEL WILDING (Akhnatan),
BELLA DARVI (Nefer), EDMUND PURDOM (The Egyptian) with
PETER USTINOV, JUDITH EVELYN, HENRY DANIELL, JOHN
CARRADINE, CARL BENTON REID, TOMMY RETIG, IAN
MacDONALD, DONNA MARTELL, MIKE MAZURKI, ANITRA
STEVENS, CARMEN De LAVALLADE, MIMI GIBSON, GEORGE
MELFORD, HARRY THOMPSON, KARL DAVIS, LAWRENCE
RYLE, TIGER JOE MARSH, MICHAEL GRANGER, PETER
REYNOLDS, DON BLACKMAN and JOAN WINFIELD.

167. White Christmas - August, 1954. Paramount. Running time:
120 minutes.
     Credits - Producer: ROBERT EMMETT DOLAN. Screenplay:
NORMAN KRASNA, NORMAN PANAMA and MELVIN FRANK.
Camera (Technicolor and VistaVision): LOYAL GRIGGS. Art
Directors: HAL PEREIRA and ROLAND ANDERSON. Editor:
FRANK BRACHT. Music: IRVING BERLIN.
     Cast - BING CROSBY (Bob Wallace), DANNY KAYE (Phil
Davis), ROSEMARY CLOONEY (Betty), VERA-ELLEN (Judy),
DEAN JAGGER (General Waverly) with MARY WICKES, JOHN
BRASCIA, ANNE WHITFIELD, RICHARD SHANNON, GRADY
SUTTON, SIG RUMAN, ROBERT CROSSON, RICHARD KEANE,
HERB VIGRAN, JOHNNY GRANT, GAVIN GORDON, MARCEL
De La BROSSE, JAMES PARNELL, PERCY HELTON, ELIZABETH
HOLMES, BARRIE CHASE, I. STANFORD JOLLEY, MIKE
DONOVAN, GLEN CARGYLE, LORRAINE CRAWFORD, JOAN
BAYLEY, LESTER CLARK, ERNEST FLATT and BEA ALLEN.

168. <u>We're No Angels</u> - June, 1955. Paramount. Running time:
106 minutes.
Credits - Producer: PAT DUGGAN. Screenplay: RANALD
MacDOUGALL, based on the play <u>La Cuisine des Anges</u> by
ALBERT HUSSON. Camera (Technicolor and VistaVision):
LOYAL GRIGGS. Art Directors: HAL PEREIRA and ROLAND
ANDERSON. Editor: ARTHUR SCHMIDT. Music: FREDERICK
HOLLANDER.
Cast - HUMPHREY BOGART (Joseph), PETER USTINOV
(Jules), JOAN BENNETT (Amelie Ducotel), ALDO RAY (Albert),
BASIL RATHBONE (Andre Trochard) with LEO G. CARROLL,
GLORIA TALBOTT, JOHN BAER, LEA PENMAN and JOHN
SMITH.

169. <u>The Scarlet Hour</u> - April, 1956. Paramount. Running time:
95 minutes.
Credits - Producer: MICHAEL CURTIZ. Screenplay: RIP
VAN RONKEL, FRANK TASHLIN and JOHN MEREDYTH LUCAS.
Camera (VistaVision): LIONEL LINDON. Art Directors: HAL
PEREIRA and TAMBI LARSEN. Editor: EVERETT DOUGLAS.
Music: LEITH STEVENS.
Cast - TOM TRYON (Marsh Marshall), CAROL OMHART
(Pauline Nevins), JAMES GREGORY (Ralph Nevans), JODY
LAWRENCE (Kathy), DAVID LEWIS (Sam) with ELAINE
STRITCH, E. G. MARSHALL, EDWARD BINNS, MAUREEN
HURLEY and NAT "KING" COLE.

170. <u>The Vagabond King</u> - September, 1956. Paramount. Running
time: 86 minutes.
Credits - Producer: PAT DUGGAN. Screenplay: KEN
ENGLUND and NOEL LANGLEY, from the operetta, music by
RUDOLF FRIML, book and lyrics by WILLIAM H. POST and
BRIAN HOOKER; and from the play <u>If I Were King</u> by JUSTIN
HUNTLEY McCARTHY. Camera (Technicolor and VistaVision):
ROBERT BURKS. Art Directors: HAL PEREIRA and HENRY
HUMBSTEAD. Editor: ARTHUR SCHMIDT. Music: RUDOLF
FRIML and JOHNNY BURKE.
Cast - ORESTE (François Villon), KATHRYN GRAYSON
(Catherine De Vaucelles), RITA MORENO (Huguette), SIR
CEDRIC HARDWICKE (Tristan), WALTER HAMPDEN (King
Louis XI) with LESLIE NIELSEN, WILLIAM PRINCE, JACK
LORD, BILLY VINE, FLORENCE SUNDSTROM, HARRY
McNAUGHTON, G. THOMAS DUGGAN, RALPH SUMPTER,
GREGORY MORTON and LUCIE LANCASTER.

171. <u>The Best Things in Life Are Free</u> - September, 1956.
Twentieth Century-Fox. Running time: 104 minutes.
Credits - Producer: HENRY EPHRON. Screenplay:
WILLIAM BOWERS and PHEOBE EPHRON, based on a story
by JOHN O'HARA. Camera (De Luxe Color, Cinemascope):
LEON SHAMROY. Art Directors: LYLE R. WHEELER and

MAURICE RANSFORD. Editor: DOROTHY SPENCER. Music:
LIONEL NEWMAN.

Cast - GORDON MacRAE (Da Sylva), ERNEST BORGNINE
(Brown), DAN DAILEY (Henderson), SHEREE NORTH (Kitty),
TOMMY NOONAN (Carl) with MURVYN VYE, PHYLLIS AVERY,
LARRY KEATING, TONY GALENTO, NORMAN BROOKS,
JACQUES D'AMBOISE, ROXANNE ARLEN, BYRON PALMER,
EUGENE BORDEN, LINDA BRACE, PATTY LOU HUDSON,
JULIE VAN ZANDT, LARRY KERR, CHARLES VICTOR, HAROLD
MILLER, EMILY BELSER, PAUL GLASS and BILL FOSTER.

172.   The Helen Morgan Story - October, 1957.   Warner Bros.-First
       National.   Running time: 118 minutes.
       Credits - Producer: MARTIN RACKIN.   Screenplay:
STEPHEN LONGSTREET, OSCAR SAUL, DEAN RIESNER and
NELSON GIDDING.   Camera (Cinemascope):   TED McCORD.
Art Director: TOM BECKMAN.   Editor: FRANK BRACHT.
Music: LARRY PRINZ.
       Cast - ANN BLYTH (Helen Morgan), PAUL NEWMAN (Larry),
RICHARD CARLSON (Wade), GENE EVANS (Whitney Krause),
ALAN KING (Ben) with CARA WILLIAMS, WALTER WOOLF
KING, VIRGINIA VINCENT, WARREN DOUGLAS, DOROTHY
KING, ED PLATT, SAMMY WHITE, WALTER WINCHELL,
JIMMY McHUGH, RUDY VALLEE, PEGGY De CASTRO,
BABETTE De CASTRO and CHERI De CASTRO.

173.   The Proud Rebel - April, 1958.   Buena Vista.   Running time:
       103 minutes.
       Credits - Producer: SAMUEL GOLDWYN, JR.   Screenplay:
JOE PETRACCA and LILLIE HAYWARD.   Camera (Technicolor):
TED McCORD.   Art Director: McCLURE CAPPS.   Editor:
AARON STELL.   Music: JEROME MOROSS.
       Cast - ALAN LADD (John Chandler), OLIVIA de
HAVILLAND (Linnett Moore), DEAN JAGGER (Harry Durleigh),
DAVID LADD (David Chandler), CECIL KELLAWAY (Doctor
Enos Davis) with THOMAS P. HARAN, HENRY HULL, ELI
MINTZ, JAMES WESTERFIELD, JOHN CARRADINE, DEAN
STANTON and THOMAS PITTMAN KING.

174.   King Creole - July, 1958.   Paramount.   Running time: 116
       minutes.
       Credits - Producer: HAL B. WALLIS.   Screenplay:
HERBERT BAKER and MICHAEL V. GAZZO, based on the
novel A Stone for Danny Fisher by HAROLD ROBBINS.
Camera (VistaVision): RUSSELL HARLAN.   Art Director:
J. MacMILLAN JOHNSON.   Editor: WARREN LOW.   Music:
WALTER SCHARF.
       Cast - ELVIS PRESLEY (Danny Fisher), CAROLYN JONES
(Ronnie), DOLORES HART (Nellie), DEAN JAGGER (Mr.
Fisher), WALTER MATTHAU (Maxie Fields) with LILLIAN
MONTEVECCHI, VIC MORROW, JAN SHEPHERD, PAUL
STEWART, BRIAN HUTTON and JACK GRINNAGE.

175. The Hangman - April, 1959. Paramount. Running time:
      86 minutes.
          Credits - Producer: FRANK FREEMAN. Screenplay:
      DUDLEY NICHOLS. Camera: LOYAL GRIGGS. Art Director:
      HAL PAREIRA and HENRY BUMSTEAD. Editor: TERRY
      MORSE. Music: HARRY SUKMAN.
          Cast - ROBERT TAYLOR (MacKenzie Bovard), TINA
      LOUISE (Selah Jennison), FESS PARKER (Buck Weston),
      JACK LORD (Johnny Bishop), MICKEY SHAUGNESSY (Al
      Cruse) with GENE EVANS and SHIRLEY HARMER.

176. The Man in the Net - June, 1959. Mirisch-Jaguar Productions.
      Running time: 97 minutes.
          Credits - Producer: WALTER MIRISCH. Screenplay:
      REGINALD ROSE, based on a story by PATRICK QUENTIN.
      Camera: JOHN SEITZ. Art Director: HILDYARD BROWN.
      Editor: RICHARD HEERMANCE. Music: HANS J. SALTER.
          Cast - ALAN LADD (John Hamilton), CAROLYN JONES
      (Linda), DIANE BREWSTER (Vickie Carey), JOHN LUPTON
      (Brad Carey), CHARLES McGRAW (Steve Ritter) with BETTY
      LOU HOLLAND, TOM HELMORE, JOHN ALEXANDER,
      KATHERINE GIVNEY, ALVIN CHILDREN, EDWARD BINNS,
      SUSAN GORDON, BARBARA BAIRD, MIKE McGREERY,
      CHARLES HERBERT and STEPHEN PERRY.

177. The Adventures of Huckleberry Finn - May, 1960. M-G-M.
      Running time: 107 minutes.
          Credits - Producer: SAMUEL GOLDWYN, JR. Screenplay:
      JAMES LEE, based on the novel by MARK TWAIN. Camera
      (Metrocolor and Cinemascope): TED McCORD. Art Director:
      GEORGE W. DAVIS and McCLURE CAPPS. Editor: FREDERIC
      STEINKAMP. Music: JEROME MOROSS.
          Cast - TONY RANDALL (The King), EDDIE HODGES
      (Huckleberry Finn), ARCHIE MOORE (Jim), PATTY McCORMACK
      (Joanna), NEVILLE BRAND (Pap) with MICKEY SHAUGNESSY,
      JUDY CANOVA, ANDY DEVINE, SHERRY JACKSON, BUSTER
      KEATON, JOHN CARRADINE, FINLAY CURRIE, JOSEPHINE
      HUTCHINSON, ROYAL DANO, PARLEY BAER, STERLING
      HOLLOWAY, DOLORES HAWKINS and DEAN STANTON.

178. A Breath of Scandal - October, 1960. Paramount. Running
      time: 98 minutes.
          Credits - Producer: CARLO PONTI. Screenplay: WALTER
      BERNSTEIN, based on the play Olympia by FERENC MOLNAR.
      Camera (Technicolor): MARIO MONTUORI. Art Director:
      GENE ALLEN. Editor: HOWARD SMITH. Music: B.
      CICOGNINI.
          Cast - SOPHIA LOREN (Olympia), JOHN GAVIN (Charlie),
      MAURICE CHEVALIER (Philip), ISABEL JEANS (Eugenie),
      ANGELA LANSBURY (Lina) with TULLIO CARMINATI,
      ROBERTO RISSO, CARLO HINTERMANN, MILLY VITALE,
      ADRIENNE GESSNER and FREDERICK LEDEBUR.

179. Francis of Assisi - July, 1961. Twentieth Century-Fox.
      Running time: 111 minutes.
          Credits - Producer: PLATO A. SKOURAS. Screenplay:
      EUGENE VALE, JAMES FORSYTH and JACK THOMAS, based
      on the book Joyful Beggar by LOUIS De WOHL. Camera (De
      Luxe Color and Cinemascope): PIERO PORTALUPI. Art
      Director: EDWARD CARRERE. Editor: LOUIS R. LOEFFLER.
      Music: MARIO NASCIMBENE.
          Cast - BRADFORD DILLMAN (St. Francis), DOLORES HART
      (Clare), STUART WHITMAN (Paolo), EDUARD FRANZ (Pietro),
      PEDRO ARMENDARIZ (Sultan) with CECIL KELLAWAY,
      ATHENE SEYLER, FINLAY CURRIE, RUSSELL NAPIER,
      MERVYN JOHNS, JOHN WELSH, HAROLD GOLDBLATT, EDITH
      SHARPE, JACK LAMBERT, MALCOLM KEEN, OLIVER JOHN-
      STON, JULE MAURO, MANUEL BALLARD, EVI MANARDI,
      UTI HOF, PAUL MULLER, JOHN KARLSSEN, DAVID MAUNSELL,
      CYRUS ELIAS, WALTER MARLOW, CURT LOWEN and RENZO
      CESANA.

180. The Comancheros - October, 1961. Twentieth Century-Fox.
      Running time: 107 minutes.
          Credits - Producer: GEORGE SHERMAN. Screenplay:
      JAMES EDWARD GRANT and CLAIR HUFFAKER, based on the
      novel by PAUL I. WELLMAN. Camera (De Luxe Color and
      Cinemascope): WILLIAM H. CLOTHIER. Art Directors: JACK
      MARTIN SMITH and ALFRED YBARRA. Editor: LOUIS R.
      LOEFFLER. Music: ELMER BERNSTEIN: Second Unit Direc-
      tor: CLIFF LYONS.
          Cast - JOHN WAYNE (Captain Jake Cutter), STUART
      WHITMAN (Paul Regret), INA BALIN (Pilar), NEHEMIAH
      PERSOFF (Graile), LEE MARVIN (Crow) with MICHAEL
      ANSARA, BRUCE CABOT, PAT WAYNE, JOAN O'BRIEN,
      JACK ELAM, EDGAR BUCHANAN, HENRY DANIELL, RICHARD
      DEVON, STEVE BAYLOR, JOHN DIERKES, ROGER MOBLEY,
      BOB STEELE, LUISA TRIAVA, IPHEGENIE CASTIGLIONI,
      AIESSA WAYNE and GEORGE J. LEWIS.

Index of Names

Underscored page numbers refer to illustrations.

Index of Titles

Underscored page numbers refer to illustrations.